LLOYD H. AHLEM

DO I HAVE TO BE ME?

THE PSYCHOLOGY OF HUMAN NEED

A Division of G/L Publications
Glendale, California, U.S.A.

Second Printing, 1974
© Copyright 1973 by G/L Publications
All rights reserved

Published by
Regal Books Division, G/L Publications
Glendale, California 91209
Printed in U.S.A.

Library of Congress Catalog Card No. 73-79843
Hardcover edition: ISBN 0-8307-0248-2
Softcover edition: ISBN 0-8307-0252-0

Contents

1 Love: a Driving Force

"Would you guys kiss me good night?" It was the last request after a long night's ordeal. A drug episode had gone bad.

The plump, but attractive and lovable, young lady arrived at our home about 11 P.M. Obviously her world had come unglued. Her words could only suggest the grotesque emotions she felt. Wracked with unexplained fear, only half knowing where she was, she had convinced a friend to drive her to our home where, hopefully, some peace might be found.

Slowly her senses returned to normal. But intermittent shrieks signaled a series of delusions, induced by hallucinogens, that erupted in her mind. Gradually we were able to "talk her down." She was "crashing" from a marijuana escapade, but the marijuana had been laced with a hard drug. The resultant trip was longer and more terrifying than she had thought possible.

Five hours passed before her mind cleared enough for her to relate accurately what was happening. We listened intently, not precisely sure how to respond, but we did know that this was a time for tender loving care. We continued giving assurance, being careful not to stimulate guilt in an already troubled mind.

About 5 A.M. she was ready for sleep. We tucked her in bed in our spare room and let her sleep around the clock.

That simple gesture of affection, the kiss good night, was the assurance that someone cared. In life's toughest spots, there is absolutely no substitute for love.

"Love makes the world go 'round, " so proclaims the ballad most of us have heard. Love is idolized, joked about, even hated. Love is the dominant theme of plays, books, and poetry. Love is fought for, suppressed, stimulated, even prostituted. Probably more human energy is expended in the various expressions and frustrations of love than in any other human experience.

Why? For some reason we were made with the need to give and to receive love. The Bible's creation story describes God's need for an affiliation—some loving relationship. So He made man. He made him in His own image with a need to love and be loved. Other world religions, as well, portray man in some kind of affiliation to his maker. Sometimes they present the relationship as positive, sometimes as negative. Christian faith, however, is always positive. It describes God as loving man so much that He gave Himself to man in order to love him supremely.

Not only do normal human experience and the religions

of mankind affirm the need for love, but also current psychological research recognizes empirically this human need. A disease called *marasmus* afflicts severely love-deprived children. The disease manifests itself in a number of physical and psychological symptoms. Physically, the affected children appear to be starving: their abdomens protrude, and their limbs are shriveled. Their complexion is devoid of vitality, and their flesh is like putty to the touch. Psychologically, they avoid all relationships with people, even the establishment of eye contact with others, and instead they occupy their attention with inanimate objects in a decreased range of interests.

Typically, marasmic children have been emotionally abandoned. Their mothers may have parked them in the unwilling care of others or left them in the hospitals where they were born. For the most part, substitute mothers tend only to minimize the child's physical discomforts. They may change his pants and offer him a bottle, but they spare him little affection. Consequently, the child senses early that he has been rejected.

According to some studies, the personalities of marasmic children who experienced prolonged emotional deprivation were damaged for life. Some were so damaged that they died from starvation while still very young. Seemingly unable to consume and utilize the food offered them, they perished. Those who survived to adolescence became withdrawn, weepy types, with little enthusiasm for normal human experience. Others developed schizophrenic personalities as adults, retreating from life, shutting out most interpersonal experience.

When a person's very survival depends on love, the need for love appears clearly established. Because love is essential to life, doctors routinely instruct nurses to fondle and caress babies and young children who may be hospitalized during the psychologically vulnerable days that come early in life. The standard prescription they inscribe on the patients' charts is "TLC"—tender loving care. Such warm attention may spare children great misery later in life.

Through meaningful love experiences, children develop emotional security and confidence in themselves. Having seen love expressed and having felt its assurance, they are able to enter fully into healthy relationships and experiences of their own. The confidence love has given them minimizes their fears of failure.

But what do we mean by the term *love?* In the English language, *love* has many different meanings. When we define love as a basic need, we had better consider which definition we are using. Some experiences that bear the label *love* are not love. Some "loving" relationships, in fact, may be very harmful. Who would prescribe a pseudo love that wounds where healing is needed? Certainly, no one has a basic need for false love. But what kind of love do we really need?

Strolling across our college campus one day, I caught just one phrase of a couple's intense conversation. "Baby," the fellow said to his girl, "I sure would love to love your skin!" Observing this half-nelson demonstration of affection, I doubted that the love he offered was a lofty altruism given for its own sake. His use of the word expressed rather his need for some reduction of a biological drive. To describe the exuberance and desire of adolescence as *love* does not make it the same as loving one's neighbor as oneself. Perhaps the term *lust* better fits the definition of love in this instance. One might seriously question whether emotional development is dependent on this type of love experience.

Just as love and lust are confused in our language, and often in our motives, so love and hostility become confused in the behavior of certain people. In a large metropolitan high school, the teachers and counselors were asked to list the names of students who had reputations for being the lovers in the student body. "Lovers" referred to youngsters

4

known for necking in public, for brashness in sexual adventure, and for general preoccupation with the opposite sex. When the composite list was completed, personality tests that had been administered to the entire student body were drawn from the files for the student lovers. One dominant trait they exhibited was hostility! The group had a greater than average history of fights on campus and conflicts with teachers; they shared a record of general irritability at school.

Our social conditioning has taught us to reject hostility in most instances. But hostile behavior, contained in the words and gestures of love, may be expressed more easily. These students had found a way effectively to disguise, yet express, their feelings. Hostility disguised as love hardly contributes to the emotional development of its recipient.

Still another definition of love that operates widely in American culture is romantic love. There can be little doubt that many people seek this type of love to bring fulfillment to their lives. Some sociologists who write about marriage have attempted to describe the nature of romantic love.

Let's look at a composite of their efforts to define the term.

1. A strong emotional attachment to a member of the opposite sex. An exclusive affectional relationship with a love partner.

2. An emotional interdependence with the person chosen as the object of one's love and affection.

3. Physical attraction and sexual desire for the loved one. A sense of stimulation in the presence of the chosen partner.

4. Strong emotional reassurance resulting from the love relationship. A sense of bolstering one's own feelings of self-worth.

5. An idealization of one's partner that actually distorts the image of the loved one. The romantic lover deliberately engages in fantasy while contemplating his relationship with his partner.

This definition of love is important for several reasons. First, many normal people hold this conception of love fulfillment. They sincerely believe in the promises of romantic love and seek to be enhanced by it. If theirs has been a healthy emotional development in the early years, they can expect that love and marriage will provide a fulfilling experience. They have observed others for whom this has been true.

Second, a reasonably large number of people enter into romantic love to compensate for some deficit in their lives. They may have been unhappy in the past, or they may have considered themselves inadequate. The prospect of a romantic experience that may answer their needs is appealing indeed. But they want this love for its therapeutic value rather than as a growth experience.

Third, in extolling romantic love, the American culture has constructed an ideal with built-in fallacies. As a result, individuals often find themselves thrown emotionally off balance. In the average marriage, the idealization process goes into reverse as married lovers discover the truth about each other. A starry-eyed husband wakes to find his wife is a witch until she has had her second cup of coffee in the morning. An adoring bride observes that her husband cares more for his own comfort than for hers. Then their strongly emotional interdependence rocks as the partners discover that they fail to meet each other's needs and expectations.

Just as man has no need for love disguised as hostility or lust, so he has no need for the kind of love implicit in the American definition of romantic love. Must a person experience this distortion of love in an attempt to meet his emotional needs? Do the benefits of romantic love so outweigh its harmfulness that we need not be greatly concerned? Or is there a better way?

Let us look now at another definition of love that we may know. This love is more positive in nature and perhaps comes closer to meeting our basic needs.

Brotherly love receives a great deal of current emphasis. For today's turmoil, perceived by almost everyone, it is the easily prescribed antidote.

In the ancient Greek language, several kinds of love were defined and distinguished from one another. The Greek concept of brotherly love involves concern for one another's welfare. It includes the idea of mutuality because this kind of love experience is discontinued, or at least jeopardized, without some agreement that the object of love will return love in kind. Both parties profit from the relationship. Because of the relationship, both are better off than each one is individually.

I recall a missionary's story of two lepers in the Orient. One had no arms; the other had no legs. Both were starving since neither could work effectively alone. The solution to their problem came when the leper who could walk carried the leper who had arms. Together they worked as one and fulfilled each other's survival needs. A warm feeling of kinship arose between them. Brotherly love existed with a kind of wholesome profit in mind. Two could do more than one if they worked together. Further, the profits extended to other areas of life. Since their relationship had solved one problem, other problems suggested themselves for solution through the same cooperation. Brotherly love can grow in depth and significance.

The price of reciprocal love, brotherly love, is the surrender of a certain portion of one's personal sovereignty. Decisions about oneself must be shared, or the relationship collapses. It is at this point that many people balk. The one who seems to need help most may be unable to accept it. The risk of surrendering a little of one's sovereignty seems too great even to accomplish simple things. As a result, the helpless one decides to go it alone, failing increasingly to meet the demands society makes on him. At best, he experiences only minimal satisfactions in life. At worst, he turns completely within himself and, psychologically, perishes.

Brotherly love seems to be so logical an answer to society's ills, yet it is so rarely applied. Is it because people believe that personal sovereignty is more important than the solution of their problems? Is the need to be sovereign in one's experience more potent than the need for love, or does withdrawal obscure needs one had best forget?

2 Love: a Developmental Sequence

We have considered briefly the need for love fulfillment. The physical survival of some youngsters depends on it. The healthy psychological functioning of all of us is impaired without it. Our discussion has indicated, however, that not all the experiences commonly called love are exactly that. We do not need love disguised as lust or hostility, we need a purer love, a refined and mature love.

The expression of mature love follows a developmental sequence. It grows from the infant's experience to adult fulfillment. While the whole person is growing, the ability to experience love is growing. Love doesn't begin in the middle of its sequence or start at both ends. It has a fairly normal progression that is identifiable. If an individual fails to attain a developmental stage properly or completely, his ability to love and to be loved is impaired. He must grow into mature love in orderly fashion.

The first step in the developmental sequence is to experience healthy, sensual love in infancy. The more I work with children the more I see the importance of healthy emotional experience early in life.

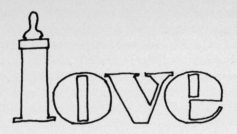

Some years ago I met a boy whose behavior was so extremely offensive that he had to be dismissed from school. He was constantly in trouble for taking off his clothes in school rest rooms or for exposing himself sexually on the playground. No amount of admonition had any effect in correcting him.

The lad was born while his father was away at war. His mother found work to support the family, which included a senile grandmother with an abrasive personality. Born in a military hospital, the boy was rushed home shortly after birth so his mother could return to work. While mother was employed nights as a cocktail waitress, grandmother supposedly kept house. Mother's job, grandmother's confusion, baby's needs, and father's absence combined to create chaos. For months the child's emotional needs were neglected. He often cried himself to sleep and was seldom cuddled and enjoyed by his mother or grandmother. He was like an abandoned child in his own home.

Father's return from the service promised some improvements. Grandmother's death simplified life at home. Father got an adequate job, though he traveled a lot, and mother came home to care for her son. One might have expected that these changes would help, but too much time had passed, and the early experiences of this child had been critical.

Realizing that her son had missed much love as an infant, mother decided to catch up somehow. She fed him, slept with him, cuddled him, smothered him. This abnormal relationship continued until he was in the fourth grade. Now we had a boy who was anxious, obnoxious, and thoroughly confused. He grew hostile—cruel to animals and highly destructive of property. One day his mother phoned. "What shall I do? He's tearing up the bathroom tile with a hammer!" The boy had sensed that he had been used to alleviate mother's guilt and was enraged by it. Finally, lengthy depth therapy and firmly controlled behavior at school alleviated the problem considerably.

What went wrong, specifically? This boy had missed the earliest stage of development of love. Babies and young children have a great need for wholesome, sensual pleasure. They require stroking, fondling, cuddling—lots of physical contact, enjoyed by both parent and child. Healthy experiences like this build self-assurance into children that protects them from hurt for years to come. But this child had been ignored. Now it was too late.

Children are highly sensitive to the attention given them though they lack words to express these feelings until years later. A placid infant placed in the arms of an emotionally disturbed adult will very often become upset and cry. Yet no words have been exchanged, and the adult believes that the child is feeling only pleasure. Warm physical handling and the accepting attitudes of happy parents seem to penetrate to the deepest recesses of children's minds, bringing emotional health and well-being. But these attentions must come early and with wholesome motives. One really cannot catch up later. Timing is all-important.

Because of early deprivation, this boy lacked the roots of emotional growth and became unsure and unstable. Then his mother compensated in a neurotic way, resolving her own guilt rather than fostering his development. He became a problem at school because he was retaliating for mother's early neglect and later neurotic compensations. Aggressive behavior became his symbolic way of resisting her smothering: perhaps misbehaving would make her stop loving in this solicitous way. The absence of the father in the service and on his job left the boy without a clear example to follow. He had never seen a model of mature male behavior at close range. Thus he had no concept of what normal behavior is like. Lacking the foundation of wholesome early experiences, this boy will continue to suffer in attempting to grow to mature love and emotional experience.

Research findings also point up the need for early, wholesome attention. From studies of children reared in institutions where early, sensual love is lacking, we know that such children exhibit at least three general kinds of problems.

First, they show delayed speech development together with a resulting lack of social graciousness. Speech development is a key indicator of early social growth. Infantile speech in older children is a symbolic plea for emotional assurance. When normally developed children hear such speech, they reject the speaking child as "babyish." Thus the deprived child is caught between his need for assurance and his need for social approval.

Second, these children display signs of general emotional impoverishment. They lack emotional spontaneity and seem cold. They tend to hide their emotions and withdraw from uncomfortable situations. In their efforts to avoid being hurt, they lose the benefits of normal social life.

Finally, they show a diminished general intelligence. The social and emotional withdrawal limits attempts at learning. Limited learning, in turn, appears as dullness on mental ability tests. We sometimes call this group of symptoms "institutionalism" or "hospitalism." Where love is diminished, so also is personal and emotional growth.

At least two factors in our history have hindered our understanding of the need for early love. First, the belief that sensual experience was basically evil was a clear setback. The impetus of Puritanism encouraged this attitude. As a result, our culture developed excessive taboos on sex and related sensual experience. But it is important to note that the taboos were possibly a response to unhealthy love fulfillments as much as to sex itself.

Some people try to *fulfill* their love needs sensually and grow no further. When adults preoccupy themselves with physical love, they can fall into the worst type of lust. They exploit the partner physically and emotionally, while focusing their fantasy life continually on sex at an animal level. But sensual love was not designed for fulfillment; it is rather a step toward greater, more mature love, and is fulfilled only in the presence of mature love.

Segments of our society have attempted to legitimatize unhealthy attempts at fulfillment. The current hedonistic Playboy philosophy is a clear attempt in this effort. Suggesting that sensual pleasure is the fulfillment rather than the beginning of healthy love experience, the Playboy is preoccupied with sex, particularly sex of the nonreproductive variety. This is becoming a classical symptom of love development terminated at a most immature level.

The second factor that hindered general understanding of the need for love resulted from the behavioristic psychology of the 1920's. In 1928, J. B. Watson dedicated a book sardonically, "To the first mother who brings up a happy child." Watson was convinced that most of the ills of man could be traced to too much friendliness and warmth from mothers. He believed that if you wanted mature adult behavior, you treated children like pocket editions of adulthood. He failed to recognize that the needs of children are qualitatively different from the needs of adults.

This attitude prevailed so strongly that government publications of the time advised against caring warmly for little children. A significant portion of the population accepted Watson's counsel. It is possible that a measure of today's adult stress results from being raised in an era of bad advice.

When the very young child has been fulfilled through simple, demonstrated love and has felt accepted, he is ready to grow in his experience. He can move on to know mutual love. The Greeks had a word for it—*phileo*. This love was described in the preceding chapter when we considered various definitions of love that exist in our culture. This is the love that the lepers knew when they helped each other overcome their respective handicaps. This is the kind of relationship that makes corporate human activity possible. People acting together in trust solve many problems and achieve many social goals. All of our credit economy is based on mutual trust and help. We can't live without mutually supporting relationships, for when they break down, society collapses.

Little children cannot tell you in words whether they have been loved or not. They lack the ability, for defining one's emotional experience is a highly abstract problem, involving a mature use of intelligence and language. This ability does not begin to function until junior-high-school years. So often the inadequately loved baby looks and acts much like the well-cared-for child. This has led some to believe that early care, therefore, is not important. But by the time that behavioral symptoms of love deprivation appear, the optimum time for that developmental stage has passed. Much work is required to repair the damage, and it is seldom done well.

Reciprocal relationships include risk. The risk comes

when we trust others to control us in part or provide for our security. We agree to do as they wish in exchange for their doing as we wish. While doing the will of another, we yield sovereignty over a portion of our lives.

It is striking to observe how difficult it is for insecure people to trust themselves to the will of another. My experience in counseling married couples has confirmed this fact many times.

Recently, a worried young wife approached me concerning the affairs she thought her husband was having with other women. When I asked her what the evidence was, she proceeded to reel off details of scattered experiences that amounted to little. For example, she was sure he took a job as a tree trimmer so he could climb up ladders and view other women in their homes. Also, she checked the odometer on his truck daily to see how far he had traveled. One day he drove six miles to trim a tree. Since it was exactly six miles to the home of a woman friend, it was obvious to her that an affair was in progress. She was sure he had violated the reciprocal agreement of marriage.

The young wife displayed obvious signs of a disturbed personality. During extended counseling, she told of her early life at home. Her mother and father were constantly in conflict, and their troubles had left her insecure and lacking in confidence. Her mother was an unresponsive woman, unable to give warmth and assurance. Her coldness produced an anxiety in the child that dominated her entire life. She feared losing her husband, so she watched his every move. In fact, he lost one good job because she phoned his employer several times a day to find out where he was and what he was doing.

Wearied by this constant overseeing, the husband slowly withdrew from his wife. He didn't realize that he was withdrawing at first, but the daily grilling about his contacts with people brought his reaction sharply to his attention. When he began to spend more time with his wife, she

15

responded by showering him with affection and sexual advances. He thoroughly enjoyed this, of course, but was aware that her motivation was suspect. She was buying him with the gestures of love. She needed to regulate him closely so that she could trust her security to his control.

People who lacked early healthy emotional development find their mutual relationships impaired. Because of lack of self-assurance, they must protect themselves by seeking to control the behavior of those who could hurt them. Since marriage is a trusting relationship, this is the place where the problems erupt most readily.

In this case, the husband was a solid citizen with a very loving concern for his wife. Through counseling he was able to live within her ability to trust, and to respond to her need for assurance. Their problems lessened as a result. The wife, seeing the renewed interest and understanding of her husband, was able to trust him a little more and relax in the greater safety she enjoyed.

This case teaches us two definite things. First, early love experiences affect mutual human relationships by producing assurance and trust. Second, as people understand their limits and live within them, they can grow. When the limits are either constantly exceeded or never tested, growth does not take place. When this husband respected his wife's emotional limits and accepted them, he was able to create a safe environment in which she could extend her trust and safely test her limits.

Attempts to control others are a frequent compensation for lack of trust resulting from lack of love. Teachers of disturbed children know this fact all too well.

One chunky little fellow was an enlightening illustration of this truth. His home had the usual history in cases of disturbed children—cold parents, a frequently absent father, severe and erratic discipline. Unsure of himself, the boy made repeated attempts to capture the attention of his teacher. Not only did he require her attention, but he insisted that she exclude all others from her care as well. He so clung to her that she felt as though she were moving in a prisoner's leg irons.

One day she finally got him occupied with art work and proceeded to help other members of the class. But in a few moments, he was interrupting her every conversation with other students. Finally she "blew her stack." She reprimanded him and hauled him off to the principal's office. Since principals often become father figures to youngsters, you can guess how this boy reacted. He was paralyzed with fear, because his father had been scaring him out of his wits at least twice a week. The principal scolded him severely and sent him back to class.

Now this chunky rascal turned into a hellion. Realizing his physical strength, he threatened everyone who crossed his path. He challenged the teacher's instructions. He threw erasers. He threw a fit. In a few short minutes, he discovered he was in control, not the teacher. Other students responded more dramatically to him than to her. No learning could take place until he permitted it. Truly, he was boss. Only firm physical control and suspension from school restored order.

How many people in the world compensate for lack of mutual love by attempts at control? How many laws are on the books because of distrust and lack of love? How many people seek political power in a quest for love fulfillment? How many troubled souls turn inward in their attentions, imposing self-controls that strangle their emotional growth? I strongly suspect that the extremely legalistic politics and belief systems of many people result from very great emotional needs.

The love experiences of mature, fulfilled people are in striking contrast to the experiences of the troubled persons just discussed. Fortunately, some quality psychological research concerns itself with fulfillment as well as deprivation.

17

In his book *Motivation and Personality,** Abraham Maslow provides us with a profile of the traits of what he calls self-actualized people. I strongly recommend his book for inspirational as well as scholarly purposes. It gives us a look at the fortunate side of life.

Self-actualized people are those who have achieved a very full development. They are not hung up in any significant way. They have fully explored their talents and applied their energies enthusiastically and efficiently to creative endeavors.

Maslow's research shows that the universal trait among self-actualizers is the ability to be accepting. For these mature individuals no scoundrel is so low that he is not a source of some benefit. The integrity of every human being is treasured. The common humanness of us all is held in deep respect.

In the love relationships of self-actualizers, there is a great desire for psychological as well as physical intimacy. Secret languages and gestures develop between couples that only they understand. Responses toward each other tend to be spontaneous, free from defenses, the tyranny of roles and inhibitions. It is unnecessary to maintain images or appearances. One can be himself completely. No energy is wasted worrying about one's self-presentation or in suppressing anxiety. So accepting of each other are these partners that they become a single personality, yet each is a fully developed individual. Each allows his partner an irreducible, autonomous integrity. Yet each feels the needs of the other as his own. Each fully enjoys the achievements of the other as his own. Attempts to control, to humiliate, or to belittle the loved one are totally unknown.

When students in my classes in mental hygiene and human development finish reading Maslow's work they come away with mixed emotions. They feel that they have

*A. H. Maslow, *Motivation and Personality* (New York: Harper and Row, Inc., 1954), pp. 203-228.

AGAPE LOVE

glimpsed a goal in life well worth pursuing, but they also wonder if such a rewarding, fulfilling experience is possible for them. Sometimes examples of lofty experience bring a sense of frustration and discouragement. My reply is: a love experience exists that fulfills man, and it is available to everyone. It is expressed in the Greek word, *agape*.

A number of years ago my father was seriously injured in a farm machinery accident. He lost the use of one arm, and his entire nervous system lost some of its resilience from the blows received. In a few short minutes, he changed from being a vigorous, healthy farmer to a retired, physically handicapped bystander.

But this event set into motion acts of love that our family will never forget. These acts began immediately after the mishap. A neighbor found him in the field and took him to the hospital. Other friends immediately took care of the dairy. Still another finished the field work he had left incomplete. They did this not for just a day or two, but for months. Until he could supervise the work of hired men, nearly everyone who knew him seemed to be a volunteer.

The important aspect of this love is that it was given without thought of return. No one asked for pay, no one suggested they were owed a favor. We all felt ourselves recipients of an unmerited love found in few places in the world today.

19

But it didn't end there either. My father became critically ill a few years later, and again the responses were immediate. Nurses volunteered for night duty during this, his last, illness. Friends changed vacation plans so they could provide transportation to special hospitals in neighboring cities. Prepared meals for the family constantly appeared on the doorstep or in the kitchen. Anything that relieved stress and eased the work load was volunteered so freely we could hardly believe it. We were witnesses to agape love translated into human behavior.

For several generations my family has lived in a community that believes profoundly in the experience of agape love. This deep concern for the needs of others has been the mode of life for many of the people. For them, agape love relationships are the usual, normal experiences!

So far, we have defined agape love by showing it in action. Let us now discuss the nature of this love more fully. Agape love is the unmerited favor of God toward all men. It characterizes the personality of God: He has given Himself unreservedly for mankind; He wills to act in man's highest interests. We understand this directly from the New Testament, for no other religion or philosophy has generated such an altruistic concept. In this, the Christian faith stands apart.

Man did not concoct the notion of agape love; he received it by acts of God toward man. Nor did God send man some abstract definition of Himself through ascetic prophets, nor permit philosophers to envision Him in dreams. Instead, He Himself became man. He felt what we feel: loved as no one ever loved before. As the apostle Paul put it, "God was in Christ reconciling the world to himself" (2 Cor. 5:19).

Man's experience of agape love is to receive and repeat the loving acts of God. Those acts are performed in the highest interests of man, without thought of reciprocation.

Thus agape love means unreserved giving of oneself for the benefit of others, even if it costs one's life.

I recently encountered a real estate broker from a Southern state. He had just come to know that he was truly the object of the love of God. The realization had so gripped his imagination that he was doing everything possible to tell others about it. The more he talked, however, the more he understood that he had better translate the love he had experienced into his everyday life. His chief thrust was to try in every possible way to provide the best housing available to people living in oppressive conditions. After several years of work in which he sustained heavy financial loss, the leaders of a dominant community action organization successfully dubbed him a racist. He was driven from his business and left the state, bankrupt.

"How does it feel to get clobbered by those you help?" queried a friend.

"It hurts," my friend replied, "but if Christ endured a cross and was unceasing in His love, I can do no less. I'm no loser in my experience!"

But agape love is more than altruistic social action, wonderful and needed as it is. It is a belief in one's personal worth because God has declared His complete interest in man.

I have been counseling recently with a young woman who is buried in depression and despair. Her marriage has gone sour, she suffers from psychosomatic illnesses, and she is dominated by a hostility that surges uncontrollably. Like so many other troubled people, she felt little love and care as a child. She was shy and afraid to trust others in mutual relationships. Loneliness set in. She sought marriage as an escape, but found it became a trap instead. Acting out her hostility toward her husband and children, she behaved in ways that would make the most callous person feel guilty. Overwhelmed by guilt, she lapsed into depression.

What has agape love to do with the needs of a troubled soul such as this? Much in every way. Agape love holds men guiltless. It does not count up their misdeeds and extract judgment or retribution. Agape love, therefore, is the direct antidote to the guilt-ridden personality. It lets you begin again without handicap.

Bit by bit agape love is soaking into this woman's personality. The other day she offered the thought, "Every once in awhile I find out it is OK to be what I am—without compensations. Sure I'm mean and troubled, but God knows the problems I struggle with. Then I feel a little more free and can trust myself to a little more relationship with my family. It comes out all right when I do. I know I need my family to forgive me, but it's easier to ask when I know all is clear between me and God."

Unlike reciprocal or mutual love, agape love is a "no risk" relationship. You never get to the place where the love has been discontinued because of some fault of yours. You are never reduced in the eyes of God because of some failing. You can't lose this love. God always continues His love toward you in spite of any trait or deed. There is never a time or place where you cannot begin again. As a result you can grow in this love without the fear and inhibition of failure.

In mutual or reciprocal love, failure markedly reduces the motivation to begin again. A few bad experiences, and one party or the other withdraws from the relationship. A couple of instances of unfaithfulness by a husband or wife may endanger a marriage. Only if agape love is brought to bear can the wounds be healed.

In fact, most of us have become so accustomed to conditional ways of relating that we impose on God the same rules we have for our relationships with each other. But when we do, we only deceive ourselves. God's remarkable love for us continues unceasingly. The apostle Paul expresses this contagious truth vividly in his letter to the

22

Roman Christians: "Who shall separate us from the love of Christ? shall tribulation, or distress, or persecution, or famine, or nakedness, or peril, or sword?" (Rom. 8:35).

Recently a young college girl, whose life was a bundle of moral mistakes and emotional hang-ups, discovered that God loved her anyway. Accepting His love and forgiveness, she shed a heavy load of guilt that had threatened to distort seriously her whole personality. The subsequent changes in her style of living were dramatic. Grades improved. Hostility subsided. Instead of belting her parents with angry accusations for past mistakes, she saw them as people in need of the same great love. They observed the change in their daughter and scarcely believed what had happened. Soon they, too, sought to know this love that remakes man.

What kind of love does man really need? In summary, he needs three kinds. He needs careful, loving, sensual fulfillment as an infant. Out of the assurance derived from being loved, he develops the ability to enter into mutual relationships. With satisfactory relationships, he works effectively, marries well, and participates constructively in society. But what man needs most is to know the redeeming experiences of agape love. We are all subject to the human failures that damage every one of us. No one is free from some hang-up. But no experience of failure removes us from the possibility of knowing the highest love of all. This love is free, unceasing, creative within us, therapeutic. To know it, we simply accept it as a gift from God, allow it to dominate our experience, and live it out in relationship to mankind, knowing that we have in Christ the perfect example to follow.

3 Agape Love as Therapy

Several years ago I met a man who returned to his home community because of the strange power of agape love. He had not been there in years—in fact he avoided the place because of the memories it stimulated.

As a youngster he had acquired a reputation for being the most obstreperous, difficult kid in town. Although bright and inquisitive, he was a rebel from his earliest days. Teachers shuddered when they recalled his presence in school. The minister of his parish also was frustrated by his antics in church activities, and finally thrust a significant experience on the boy. In the mind of the lad, it was a totally uninvited experience.

One Saturday morning, the confirmation class of junior high schoolers had gathered at the church for their weekly lesson. Forced to attend, our budding Dillinger made the situation as difficult as possible. He challenged every rule, interrupted every student's recitation, and created chaos until class was dismissed. But on this particular day, out of sheer exasperation, the pastor declared: "Son, I am at my wits' end with you. I can bear you no longer. You cannot come back to this class. But remember, I am going to pray for you *every day* that you are alive!"

Delighted at his release, the boy skipped away and was never seen at church again. Apparently the boy's goal had been to force the minister to reject him. Since he wasn't worried about prayers following him, he considered his relationship to the world of religion effectively terminated.

Life proceeded normally for our rascal. It was a race to see whether he could get through school before the school got through with him. Completing school and seeking adventure, he entered military service shortly before World War II. Adventure he found, experiencing more military combat than most men. But the dangers of war did not seem to nudge him even a little in the direction of the church, or anything or anyone religious.

Following the war, life returned to normal. Our friend had calmed a good deal now; in fact, he had become somewhat reflective. Although he had not thought about the pastor's promise in many years, it had lain dormant deep within his mind. One quiet evening, with no uncommon stimulation present, he began to weep.

"Why am I bawling?" he muttered to himself. "I have nothing to be sad about!" It angered him that his emotions should have slipped out and caught him unaware. "Could it be really true that damned preacher is still praying? How stupid can you get?"

As he fought to control his feelings, the rudiments of his much-resisted religious education returned to his memory. "Unceasing love is ours, never stopping because of any hindrance from us," he dimly recalled the words of the monotone cleric. The words were not very persuasive when he first heard them. Why should they bug him now? But they stuck in his mind, the center of his attention.

26

AGAPE LOVE

"God, if that is so, You're on!" he shouted out loud. "If all these years have not turned You away from me, You deserve the courtesy of a real test."

Simple, unrestrained joy filled the heart of Mr. Rebel. Just for curiosity, he decided to call the old preacher, if he hadn't been planted under the daisies yet. Sure enough, he found him by tracking him through relatives he could locate.

"Are you still praying, preach?" he shouted into the phone without identifying himself.

"If you are who I think you are," returned the old minister, "I haven't missed a day since that last confirmation class."

"Well, I just wanted to let you know you've won," said our friend. Together they wept for joy and shared the greatness of agape love.

The minister was unceasing in his prayers, expecting no reciprocation and no satisfaction when he declared his intention to pray that frustrating day years ago. He would pray no matter what. And that's the way it is when God announces He will love you—no matter what.

There was a joyful reunion in the old home town a few weeks later. The young man's experience led to a renewed fellowship between the pastor and the family, and a re-created relationship among members of the family. Love and forgiveness broke past tensions and led to the exhilaration of new, genuine care.

Let's review the nature of agape love. First, you can't shut it off. It is unceasing, unbroken, unconditional. It continues even if you shut down your perceivers and fail to recognize it. It is a no-contingency relationship. It cannot be bartered, nor purchased, nor earned. It is given freely for our acceptance.

Second, agape love is inconsistent with impurity, hurt, reprisal, or destructiveness. It is uncontaminated by false motive or any other human frailty. As such, it is completely consistent with integrity, growth, openness, awareness, acceptance, and fulfillment.

Most of all, it is personal. It is God becoming man,

identifying completely with him, and regarding him as an heir to all His creation, a joint-heir with His Son. Instead of trying to keep all the adjectives I've mentioned in your head, just think of four words: unceasing, unearned, integrating, personal. If you can manage these, you will have a handy stimulus to refresh your memory.

Human pride may tempt you to forego this simple but marvelous gift. You may have developed well enough through your human successes to think you can make it on your own. If this is the case, here are some thoughts to ponder.

To make a point, let me suggest some ways to keep this love from taking you over. These methods are not uncommon; they hold the attention of a majority of the world's population. Some of the methods are downright attractive. They fatten the ego, puff up the vanity, and let you live in self-conceit. Can you think of anything more delicious?

One of the most acceptable ways of resisting love is to become excessively moral. You can become so upright, clean and dignified that you will earn barrels of social approval. You may be so trusted that you will be elected to public office to end political corruption. Or you may become the dispenser of social and moral judgment in the community. Think of the thrill of censoring movies, hunting down graft in the sanitation department, or being chairman of the citizens' committee to aid the local school in its program to teach moral and spiritual values!

Your image will be impeccable. Successfully comparing your virtues to the qualities of others, you will convince yourself that God will have to accept you. Certainly all this goodness will establish a relationship with Him. His love will be unnecessary in bringing you together; you can buy your relationship with good behavior. His concern for you and His care will then be useless, and part of His nature will be meaningless. And to declare the nature of God to be meaningless is the height of rebellion and heresy.

Morality may get you to think you are about as good as they come. Further, morality can become your effective self-defense and source of pride. It can smother your need for personal knowledge of God and His love. You will set yourself up as an idol to be emulated—a little god. But if being moral is an essentially defensive activity, and not a symptom of healthy growth, it will build a barrier between you and the needs of others. For any large measure of defensiveness in our personalities shuts us off from human need. We grow unaware because we are preoccupied with ourselves, our situation and our images. As a result we are no longer open to people. We no longer sense their needs.

Morality is another crutch we rely on to prove our worth. It becomes a substitute for the highest value that can be placed on man—his value as the personally loved creature of God.

Of course, morality is rejected by some. In rejecting it, people state that they are unwilling to be satisfied with a substitute for true worth and adequacy. But turning to immorality, they find no better answer. They only bring on themselves the scorn of the majority, and perhaps destroy themselves with guilt.

Morality ought to be motivated by the adequacy that springs up in the heart of one who fully senses he is God's own. It should be a by-product of fulfilled experience, not the means to love or adequacy. Out of the enriched sense of worth that agape gives, the motive to disciplined living can operate without raising one's defenses, and without closing one's personality to human need or restricting the sense of fulfillment.

Another, and even more acceptable, way of refusing love is to become very religious. We live in a land where church membership is popular and being religious gets you somewhere. It lines you up with the majority. Whatever else people may say about you, they can point to your religiousness if they are seeking a positive attribute to mention in your eulogy. Further, you may think that you can prove your worth to God by your religiousness and by His love.

Several years ago, I counseled with a girl who seemed to pursue both ways of attempting to forego agape love. She was *both* moral and religious. This also made her impossible! Acting out her fancied holiness, she became highly unpopular at school, though she was an attractive looking girl. No matter what topic she discussed with her schoolmates, she could not resist making moral judgments and religious pronouncements. No issue nor person was exempt from her judgments. Since her behavior led others to believe that she saw herself as superior, everyone withdrew when she appeared.

The effect of her efforts resulted in serious loneliness. In a short time she was isolated from nearly all her peers. The only people who seemed to approve of her were her sanctimonious elders.

About the time the problem became critical, a new boy moved to town and began to attend the same church. Happily she discovered that he, too, was both moral and religious. What happy communion resulted! These two unwitting youngsters shared the same personality distortions, and loneliness had driven them together. Sharing their heavenly neurosis, they fell quickly and deeply in love.

About six months later, reality came crashing through. The girl was pregnant, and her boyfriend denied any responsibility for her condition. He changed churches, never admitting guilt. Their relationship was immediately severed, as were many other friendships. People took sides concerning the young man's character. Obviously the girl was guilty, but people were strongly divided in their opinions of the boy. After all, how could such a religious and moral young man get involved in this way?

Through floods of tears and a broken heart, the girl's experience turned out to be redemptive. She recognized that she was depending upon her image of morality and religiousness for her sense of worth. Having lost her mask of respectability, she was forced to rely totally on the love of God—the God who did not falter in His concern when she got into difficulty. God accepted her because He loved her, not because she was moral and religious. Though she still bears the scars of a bitter lesson, today she is more free of defensiveness than ever before. She is open to the needs of people and has begun to relate in accepting ways and in genuine concern for her friends.

The young man, on the other hand, able to escape the immediate consequences of the problem, further reinforced himself in acceptability. He entered the ministry, and if you ever want to hear a thundering sermon on morality, I can recommend a church for you to attend. Though no one knows for sure, this young man may have found it necessary to distort the whole world to protect his own image—an image he manufactures in an attempt to convince God that he is acceptable.

Still another way to shut down your love receivers is to become very intellectual—not necessarily intelligent, just intellectual. If you are accustomed to critical thinking as we try to teach it in college, this approach should be natural for you. Just start by assuming that all information that exists is within the limits of human understanding. Believe that the human brain is all we need to understand God, ourselves, our reasons for existing. Next, assume that knowledge is expanding so fast that all information worth understanding is known now or lies just beyond the next issue of your favorite scientific journal. Then it is only a matter of time until all these puzzling questions about the meaning of life, about God, or about religious experience are exposed to the light of science, when they will convert to simple psychological, sociological, or scientific principles. Don't be caught admitting that there may be truth existing and available through something as unhuman as divine revelation.

You may have to get a little stubborn about it, occasionally. You are sure to meet someone who insists otherwise. Further, he will declare that he has found a great sense of certainty and personal peace in his faith. He actually seems to enjoy God! What's more, he made his discovery without being very bright. But if you insist on limiting your understanding to things experimentally perceived, you can dispose of him in a few uncomfortable minutes. After all, what you can't see can't possibly be real. Problems that don't fit your notions of experimental verification can't possibly exist. By fiat rule them out! Or at least rule them out of your mental order.

I should warn you about one psychological phenomenon, however. It is called perseveration. When you are sitting by your fireplace following a day of occupational fulfillment at the local loan office, thoughts may erupt without apparent stimulation. This is perseveration. While staring into the flames from the old Yule log, questions about the meaning of life, God and supreme love may sneak up on you. You may wonder, "How do I know that I am *not* the object of great love? What tests could I make to prove this negative hypothesis? Suppose it *is* true that God regards me as worth His supreme efforts to reach me. What then?"

If you are a good intellectual in the defensive, personal sense of the word, you will crush such thinking and relegate it to the mental trash heap. There's no sense facing up to what might be reality when you can protect yourself. Return the old noodle to the sand of uncertainty. Science encompasses all.

One final method of fending off agape love is worth considering. It is a method employed by multitudes today. It is "in." To some degree, it is replacing the intellectual style that is going out of vogue.

This method bears several different names. Turning on, blowing your mind, grooving are some of the young people's terms for it. Getting loaded, stoned, gassed, or lubricated were the words used when I was in college and engulfed in lower-middle-class status. Now that I'm educated in upper-middle-class status it is called transcending, existentially experiencing, or momentarily savoring. No matter, it is all an exploration of the emotions to see how much and how varied human mental experience can be. It is similar to turning up the juice in any complex jungle of electronic circuitry to see all the funny sparks.

Man seems determined to avoid the boring, the mundane. Even if it damages his biological or psychological makeup, he seeks for the experience that stretches human sensation. He feels that if he has explored human capacity for experience to the fullest, then life may be worth something.

To make effective use of this method of substitution for supreme love, you must start with the same assumptions as does the intellectual. You must be your own validating source and limit human experience to your own terms of understanding. You must exclude the possibility of experience that has a divine origin. Try to do that which freaks you out at the moment. Once more hide the noggin in the basket and breathe deeply. What you can't see isn't there. It is only what you feel that counts. And surely you can generate an emotional, perceptual freak-out that compares well with agape love. Certainly there must be some humanly contrived sensation that approaches what God can do in you!

You will have to avoid studiously the testimony of the

apostle Paul when he declares, "What no man ever saw or heard, what no man ever thought could happen, is the very thing God prepared for those who love him" (1 Cor. 2:9). This is the ultimate challenge. It flatly declares there is no equal to agape love. You will have to find this assertion to be either true or false. There is no middle ground.

The possible thought that there *is* an integrating experience available as a gift that maximizes human existence and provides infinite knowledge and guidance for life may throw you off course considerably. You might not enjoy your next experience of turning on, or getting high, knowing that a better alternative is possible, one without the tragic consequences to body and mind.

My point is this. Agape love originates *outside* of human experience, so it is not restricted by human limits of perception or understanding. To fully experience it, we must be open to the simple fact that it is given away freely and requires no striving. God gave it in the form of a person, Jesus, who can live within us. As we open ourselves to Him, we must set aside our favorite alternatives and our most limiting, though delicious, sins.

The best news any of us can receive is that agape love affirms man and declares him worthy. You don't need defenses, polish, morality, intelligence, religiousness. You need a person. When you have Him who is love, He may lead you to these virtues. But they are no substitute for Him.

When you choose to see yourself as God sees you, and let these perceptions dominate your mental experience, a sense of worth and adequacy will begin its stalwart growth in your being. Man is affirmed, not denied by love. "God so loved the world . . ." (John 3:16).

Can you consciously make the choice to receive this love and forgiveness, to supplant whatever substitute you have stuck in its place? When you do, you will begin the greatest adventure in life. You will begin to experience unbartered relationships and enjoy the openness that comes when defensiveness ceases.

People who have little need to protect themselves psychologically lead the most enjoyable lives. They are free to experience relationships fully and free to be empathetic to need. They spend little energy maintaining arsenals of automatic responses to perceived threats.

In one office where I worked, a number of secretaries shared a large working space. Since I passed them each morning as I came to work, I would say hello and josh a bit before getting down to business. One morning, though, I made a serious mistake. I gaily greeted each of them as I passed, except for one who was hidden behind the Multilith, cleaning ink off the floor. About thirty minutes later a sobbing lady, with insult stabbing her psyche, came blubbering into my office. "Why didn't you speak to me?" she muttered. "Am I so small in your eyes that you won't even say good morning?"

"Did I miss greeting you, Harriet? What a shame to start a day without savoring your smiling face!" I thought I was being humorous, but the sarcasm missed nobody. "I'm sorry," I continued. "It will never happen again."

As I considered what I knew about Harriet, I realized that she had a reputation for extreme selfishness. She carefully guarded her interests. She was offended when the telephone was placed an inch or two farther away from her than from the secretary who shared it. She took a day of sick leave when the title of her job was mistakenly entered in an official document as "clerk" rather than "secretary."

It is no accident that protective, defensive people are seen as snobbish, or selfish, or both. They become so preoccupied with the need to prevent hurt that they spend

36

all their energies building defense mechanisms and repertoires of retorts to fend off hurt. Selfishness and protectiveness become the same process. Self-centered people see themselves as protective, but others see them as selfish. And the result is a life almost completely shut off from others.

Although she was physically attractive and a capable employee, Harriet had a continuing problem keeping a job. I also learned that a few years previous to my acquaintance with her, she had been divorced by her husband on the grounds of mental cruelty. Then slowly a change began to take place.

A pastor who saw her as a hurting individual, rather than a selfish snob, began to show her a new set of perceptions that she could choose. Day by day she grew in the understanding that much of her armor was needless because she could experience agape love—love that was free and without threat. He directed her to people who had also experienced this love, and from them she learned what this love means in human experience.

Several years later she was able to chuckle about that weepy day when I had failed to say good morning and she hurt so miserably. She proved that when love comes in, defenses drop. Freedom begins, fatigue moves out. A refreshed energy is available that once was dissipated in self-protection, for protection further removes us from people and heightens our need to defend ourselves. Our efforts can become a vicious circle until our energies are sapped and we have to be tucked away for awhile with a nervous breakdown. Harriet had broken the cycle. She had found resources outside herself and in other people. Healing had begun.

If people have not developed the basic types of love, their defenses are often so elaborate and raised so high that it is difficult to communicate agape love to them by either word or deed. Approaches must be carefully made, or they will be scared away from examining agape love. In any new experience their first order of business is self-defense. With some, you feel as though you have to survey carefully their personal Maginot Line of emotional fortifications and find a way to sneak around it just to get acquainted.

Or you may sense that they have their antennae protruding in all directions, fearfully awaiting the slightest static. With emotional amplifiers turned up high, they perceive every garbled message and react with danger signals. They seem to anticipate getting hurt at any moment. It is a horrible way to live, and it is unnecessary.

Once in awhile, however, the frightened mind is willing to take the risk of experiencing agape love. Instead of settling into discouragement, the person dares at last to trust again. Out of desperation, he finds peace. But ideally, I think that a child should be able to grow in such a way that, as a natural step in his developmental sequence, he enters into God's great love for him.

Agape love affirms man. An affirmed person can afford to be less defensive. With defenses down, he reaches out to others, fully sharing life. This is why I feel that any therapeutic experience we can offer people will help open the way for agape. Any reduction of tension we might bring about, any soothing of troubled minds, is a most valuable experience.

Pure love secures the person as you have discovered if you have accepted God's love for you. Because you know that you are of infinite worth and the object of unceasing love, you move with a new sense of confidence and peace. Your most stubborn feelings of inferiority crumble away. Now that your guard is down, it is possible for you to savor a wider range of your inner experiences. Since you are no longer rejecting your feelings and fighting for the control of your emotions, your subconscious mind frees itself. Mental garbage stored for years beneath your level of awareness may come to light.

A handsome young man began asking me about some strange feelings he was having. He was an intelligent, successful, high-school teacher whose interests in mental health had quickened because of students' problems as well as his own reactions.

He described symptoms of shortness of breath and of an accelerated heartbeat when the situation did not require it. They usually occurred while he was sitting quietly at home or in an audience surrounded by many people. The symptoms frightened him at first, but they subsided shortly after they appeared.

I asked him to tell me some things he believed were significant experiences in his life. He told me that his mother had died in childbirth and that he never knew her personally. When he was still very young, his father had married his mother's sister. She was truly mother to him, and he sensed no loss because of the death of his real mother.

His dad, however, proved to be a stern and bitter man. The boy never knew why, but he was raised with the strictest and most unfeeling discipline possible. Any wish he expressed or privilege he requested was denied. It soon became safer not to ask. If anything went wrong at home, he was made to feel at least partly responsible. As a result, fear of reprisal and guilt stalked him at every turn. He learned to feel guilty even in situations where he was completely innocent.

His stepmother seemed to have a good sense of balance, and while not irritating the old curmudgeon, she gave her stepson much of the assurance he needed. The lad's response was to become an exceedingly good boy. With it he bought the mother's kindness and some freedom from his father's unreasonable demands.

Through the help of a minister, the young man early learned to know the love of God. With this resource, he could resist his father's efforts to induce guilt in a good boy simply to control him.

Arriving at maturity with a sense of personal adequacy and a balanced perspective on his father, his symptoms began to appear. The question that puzzled him was: "Why these troublesome feelings when I'm at the peak of my life and doing better than ever before? Am I becoming sick?"

My suggestion was that he ought to regard his feelings as symptoms of healing, rather than of illness. He was now a mature person, open and honest with people and enjoying it. Probably the subconscious mind was just now getting around to unloading some of its stress. Our minds occasionally seem to employ time delay as a means of protection. They wait until some time when we can handle the matter, to let us know what they are doing. In a few months, the symptoms this man experienced disappeared entirely and have not returned.

I have heard other people tell of similar experiences. One young woman confessed: "When I dared to open myself to real love and the assurance it brings, I perceived more fear than ever before. But I soon discovered it was fear leaving, not entering, so I quit fighting it and gave it a grand send-off!"

We learned to know another old gentleman who had a reputation for eating nails to feed his personality, but who began to let love capture him when nearly eighty years old. The change was so dramatic that most people who heard about it didn't believe it. While speaking to a Sunday School class one day, he publicly confessed: "More things hurt me now than ever before. I have just awakened to what hurt is all about. For this I am eternally grateful."

When we are no longer perpetually on guard, the sub-conscious mind begins to speak. "Perfect love casts out fear" (1 John 4:18). When we sense that we are growing in love, experiencing certainty of self, and becoming more open to people, we can be reasonably assured that these symptoms are indicative of healing processes. Love is the great healer, the balm that refreshes the troubled soul. Love releases us to an authentic experience of ourselves and of the needs of others.

4 Seeing Oneself as an Adequate Person

Insights into human personality often come when one least expects them. Such was the case one smoggy, cold morning in Los Angeles when I boarded an airplane to attend a meeting in Chicago. With awarenesses clouded by a half-comatose condition, I was grousing through my breakfast, which for some reason had been served before we took off. Finishing my cereal, I tried to negotiate a particularly slippery orange slice when a jolt of the aircraft startled me. The orange became the property of the ash tray instead of being impaled on my fork. My awarenesses quickened as I wondered what was shaking this behemoth of the airways.

Apparently, other passengers were equally curious. Subliminal calculations began to click in our brains. What kind of force is necessary to jolt a Boeing 707, especially when the weight is applied so near the center of the cabin? Looking up, we saw a one-in-a-million specimen of humanity clogging the doorway.

At a height of about five feet, sixteen inches, she must have been able to crush elephant scales. Further, she loaded her avoirdupois into tiny shoes with pinpoint heels that were popular a few years ago. More subliminal calculations took place. How many pounds per square inch were crunching the frame of our aluminum bird with each step? Probably only a few tons, but now even the airplane was griping, and for good reason. An aeronautical engineer once told me that normally proportioned women in high heels do more damage to airplanes than all the storms over the Rockies. I was sure we would all disappear into the baggage compartment below.

As the stewardess improvised dance steps to manipulate herself down the aisle, we observed more details: a beehive hairdo with a tiny hat on top; a dark green knit suit that bulged unstylishly. Her face told us which was front and which was rear. She looked like something constructed by a wrangling committee with a big budget.

The man seated in front of me turned and muttered, "Get a load of that!"

"No thank you," I replied. "I think she has decided to sit on someone else."

I was no longer sleepy. I began to think in psychological terms—a habit that keeps me from embarrassing myself when human tragedy stimulates laughter. Now sobered, I pondered this woman's personal grief. How many barbs had she experienced? How many hours of unhappiness had she suffered? Then, how did she see herself? or explain her appearance to herself?

Phenomenological psychology tells us that we tend to behave consistently with the way we see ourselves. If you want to predict what a person will do, find out what picture or image he has of himself. If we view ourselves as adequate people, we have an attitude of self-confidence. We feel good about ourselves. On the other hand, people with a sense of inferiority look and behave the part.

If our self-view is terribly uncomfortable, we distort our images of ourselves and act "out of character," as this woman had done. Most distortions are improvements of the true image. We fancy ourselves better than we are. Or we deny that our less acceptable characteristics exist by not reacting honestly to them. After all, it is common knowledge that large, bulky people should not wear knit suits, high heels, or hats atop beehive hairdos. Yet we have seen people whose dress emphasized every fault of figure and feature. Perhaps this woman thought: If I wear a knit suit, people will know that I don't think of myself as fat, so they won't think that way of me either. Therefore it is all right to wear a knit suit, high heels, beehives, or whatever. So she distorted the self-perceived image into acceptability.

Human thinking tends to follow a number of specific rules, which have been detailed by students of cognitive behavior. In their book *Individual Behavior,* Professors Arthur Combs and Donald Snygg discuss the principles of self-perception and their relationship to self-image. Following is a discussion of some of the principles.*

Man sees himself in essentially positive, self-enhancing ways. Unless people think well of themselves, they become discouraged. To see oneself as continually failing or as continually unworthy leads to great unhappiness. Morale

*Arthur Combs and Donald Snygg. *Individual Behavior,* rev. ed. (New York: Harper and Row, Inc., 1959), p. 240.

is maintained by positive self-images. The worthwhileness of life depends on good self-perceptions. As a result, we will automatically attempt to maintain a good image even if we must distort reality to do so.

A few years ago, a certain young man became nationally known for his boxing exploits. His picture was prominently displayed in numerous papers and magazines. He had appeared in international amateur events and achieved an outstanding record. Observers predicted great success for him in professional boxing. As predicted, the young man evolved into a first-class professional fighter. Developed carefully by a skillful manager, he won matches repeatedly. In a few short years, he emerged as the world champion of his weight division.

But now, problems began to appear. Because he had lived so long with the self-picture of a champion, he began to dread defeat. He had held his title several years when these fears came to dominate him. He knew age was slowing him somewhat and that he could never fully regain the abilities of more youthful days. Gradually his personality turned inward. He avoided his friends, the press and even most friendly conversational contacts. Hating to face the world, he employed disguise artists so that he could move freely in the streets without being noticed. He had no more worlds to conquer, and the empire he owned was threatened frequently by young aspirants. Finally he became sullen and sour, and his wife divorced him.

After refusing a number of challenges to his title, he realized that he must face the possibility of defeat or be dethroned by default. One day, an improbably young upstart challenged his title. Accepting this challenge seemed to the champion to be an easy way to maintain prestige, so the fight was on. He prepared badly, and the fight showed it. He fought as though he were already defeated. His moves were halting and badly timed. In the second round, a crushing uppercut caught his chin, and he was

46

counted out. The championship was gone, and a shaky self-image was finally completely shattered.

Very likely, the fear of loss defeated him long before his final match. From that time on, he turned in his loneliness and self-disrespect to dissipation and died a pauper. Even the way of death was a confirmation of his self-perception. Seeing himself as worthless, he acted accordingly and hastened his demise.

The boxer's story shows how desperately people struggle to fend off loss of image. The need for the image to be protected constitutes a fundamental mental health problem. Many business and professional organizations no longer fire the tired and spent executive. They appoint him a vice-president on a consulting basis. We say that he is kicked upstairs. This has become the humane way of dealing with loss of ability or prowess. It preserves the man's self-esteem and still allows his useful talents to be applied.

Children, too, know the need for a good self-picture. The child who continually fails in school does not accept his failure with smiles. Instead he becomes a behavior problem. If teachers reinforce poor images, even the smallest children often respond with rebellion. Obstreperous resistance is actually a sign of vigor and insistence on personal worth. It is the emotionally sick kids who smile and retreat when repeatedly dubbed incompetents in school. A crisis arises, however, when a child becomes a threat to an instructor's need for a good self-image as a disciplinarian. School teachers usually win most of these image battles. The child's psyche generally gets axed first!

So we struggle to see ourselves in essentially positive ways. If distortion of self-image is necessary, we resort to it. We prize our self-perceptions and psychological integrity more than our sanity. When the human mind perceives too much threat, it will resort to psychotic symptoms if necessary. Mental illness is best thought of as the most efficient available means of preserving integrity.

But we see the protective processes in milder form, too. We all have ways of distorting ourselves into more comfortable images. The older a man gets, the faster he could run as a boy, or, with each passing year, the farther he used to walk to school, through deeper snow, to be taught by sterner teachers. Likewise, as I advance in years, the more significant I judge my contributions to the world to be. The meaner I become, the more I blame my family for their lack of consideration. We automatically tend toward self-aggrandizement to fulfill our need for an adequate self-concept.

Note that again we are discussing reciprocal relationships or mutual love. We discover that in our contacts with people this great need for esteem is negotiable. We trade opportunities for enhancement of our self-images. We rely on others to help us not hurt us. If you keep your agreement with me, you will enhance me and not hurt me. If I do not keep my agreement with you and hurt you, you will withdraw your favors and compliments from me. I will allow you to maintain a good image of yourself as long as you allow me to feel good about myself. This leads us to the second rule in self-perception.

The self-image I perceive is a reflected image. It is constructed from the reflections of myself that I obtain from others. As I behave in the presence of others, they respond to me with pleasantness or discomfort, or some mixture of the two. As I accumulate years of these reactions I form a picture of myself. The responses of others provide clues to what I am. I know whether I am acceptable or not by the composite picture I devise in my mind.

Here is a little experiment for you to try. Shut your eyes tightly and say the name of a well-known friend. What do you see? A clear image or a foggy one? Because our minds instantly recall pictures or images of familiar persons, no doubt the image was clear. We easily identify these people by some of their prominent features. Try it again, naming a popular public personality. What do you see?

I have frequently asked my classes to try this experiment when we discuss self-image and its problems. Class members close their eyes and I say the letters "JFK." Before his assassination students described a young, vibrant politician with a shock of hair flying in the breeze. Then came the tragedy of President Kennedy's death. The experiment was never quite the same after that. Images were more sedate. Mixed emotions accompanied the figure perceived. The somber days of the funeral often come to mind. Our perceptions were significantly modified by that unfortunate death.

Now let's go back so you can try the experiment again. Close your eyes and say your own name slowly to yourself. What do you see? Is the image as clear as the image of your friend or of the well-known public figure? Probably not. Strangely, we see ourselves indirectly through reflected images, but we see others directly. Therefore our self-images are often unclear. Also, if we need protection from the truth about ourselves, the picture will be more out of focus.

We have two great social institutions that give us more reflected images than any other. These are our families and our schools. When a child is accepted and loved at home, the family reflects these feelings on the child. Consequently, the child early sees himself as wanted and valued and likes himself. If the family sees him as ugly or a nuisance, this too will be reflected and he will see himself as unworthy or undesirable. Then he will act out his self-perceptions with rebellion or withdrawal.

When a child enters school, he must deal with an entirely new set of reflections. He is unknown in school and must establish an image of himself in this new situation. At first he automatically expects school to reflect the same picture his family has furnished him. This expectancy sometimes stimulates remarkable revelations.

Billy was the grandson of one of the elementary school principals in a district near our home. Billy was also the apple of his family's eye. He was the only grandson, and due to unfortunate circumstances there would never be another one. Billy first visited school when he was about three. Healthy, handsome, and full of spirit, he was paraded before the faculty. Every evidence of brilliance was especially noted and vignetted for the boy and any observers who could be corralled.

Then came the day when Billy enrolled in grandmother's school. He was placed with a fine teacher, and academic history was supposed to begin. But Billy would have none of it. Reading readiness became an intellectual hurdle the size of quantum physics. Simple arithmetic had to be delayed until Billy's computer developed some more. In his frustration, he took to sliding all over the floor or daydreaming when confined to his desk. How was the teacher to inform dear Grandmother principal? After all, the teacher's image and reputation were at stake, too!

After many uncomfortable discussions about Billy's quality of performance, the principal called in a psychometrist. He would give a test of intellectual competence and settle the matter—that Billy was just as bright as Grandmother believed and not as incompetent as the stubborn first-grade teacher thought him to be! But the test refused to cooperate. It declared Billy to be about as bright as most kids who have little zest for learning—somewhat below average.

When the testing was over and the results made known, the poor examiner had to endure the projected rage of an insulted grandmother and mother, too. The psychometrist had destroyed an image. He had changed the life picture of an innocent little fellow. How could he be so cruel?

50

As time went by, continual evidence showed Billy to be a simple, slightly dull little boy who would have to survive schooling as most of us do. But the problem was not over. Billy had to get his self-picture straightened out, too. No more reports of academic eminence would be projected for him. Gone were the promises of a free ride through law school financed by Grandmother's estate. No more lavish feedback about being brainy. Billy would have to get his self-picture to match the real-world picture. Though this was bound to produce stress, the sooner it happened the better, which leads us to the third rule about self-perceptions.

The individual seeks congruence between the way he sees himself and the way the world sees him. One of the problems of the seriously disturbed personality lies in his inability to see himself accurately. One Sunday afternoon I attended a worship service in a Midwestern mental institution. The patients attended voluntarily, and it appeared that those more religiously inclined dominated the meeting. Midway through the proceedings, a gentleman rose and announced that he was a prophet of God. He boldly proclaimed, "Hear me, or dire consequences will occur if you refuse my message."

His discourse was rambling and nonsensical, but we all pretended to take it in. Obviously our view of this patient differed from his view of himself. If this man were to recover a normal mental experience, his self-image would have to undergo major modifications.

Another example of the congruence problem came to my attention when a very lovely young woman sought my counsel. She was receiving so much attention from attractive men that she was in a state of anxiety about how to respond. That's a problem, I hear you say? Yes, it was, even though lots of girls would love this kind of attention. But as she revealed her history, her anxiety was easily understood.

51

This woman had been born with an ugly birthmark that covered most of one side of her face. As a growing youngster, others constantly called attention to this unsightly disfigurement. She was required endlessly to explain her appearance. Gradually her life become dominated by this unfortunate blemish. Self-rejection tempted at every moment. To compensate for intense feelings of inferiority, she used her brain, which proved to be a most efficient lever to balance the pressures on her life. Intelligent and hard working, she achieved honor student status in nearly every school she attended. But the stares and questions never ceased. Eventually her feelings got the best of her. She longed to hide and avoid people. Anything to avoid the painful, never-ending inquiries!

After high school she was employed as a secretary by a large corporation. Hoping to hide herself in work, she again compensated by using her brain. Because she worked diligently, out of sheer habit, she soon became the most successful person in her unit. She was promptly rewarded with a promotion and more responsibility. But now her inferiorities began to smother her again. Her larger number of personal contacts and duties stimulated such great fear that it threatened to drive her out of the office. She felt unable to handle her feelings about her appearance among so many people. Yielding finally to the painful emotions, she quit work and went to college, hoping to hide among the masses of students.

She reasoned that her brain had worked for her before, and that it would probably work for her again. It did. She obtained recognition for most outstanding scholarship. Invited to join honor societies, she was again thrust into the public eye and into many social contacts. The fears rose once more. She quit school and returned to work. You can guess the next sequence of events. Once again hard work and success thrust her into prominence in her business. Once again, success, the social contacts, and the fear they stimulated drove her out of the office and back to school.

Determined not to get caught in her series of compensations again, she decided to become a teacher of little children. Certainly a group of second-graders couldn't threaten anyone! But once more she had to survive academic success. She graduated magna cum laude, but the prospect of hiding in elementary school with safe little tots made the experience bearable.

Being an able student and worker helped her become an able teacher. After two years of outstanding work, she was notified that her classroom would become a demonstration class. She panicked! Hordes of teachers would be coming to observe! Supervisors, principals, consultants, and state officials would descend upon her classroom! She was back in the public eye! The old emotions of threat and fear arose once more. The school year could not end soon enough. Once more she quit!

By this time she had saved enough money to afford the surgery that would allow her to enjoy a normal appearance. At the time of our counseling session, I noticed only the slightest scar on her cheek. She was actually beautiful.

Believing that her changed face would change her self-image, she thrilled at the prospect of a normal life. But a new problem emerged, the problem that prompted her to seek professional counsel. Never before had she been asked for a date. Never had she found it necessary to fend off the advances of solicitous males. What should she do now?

Much of my advice was merely practical advice about how to play the romantic game. Our culture has devised intricate little rules for this phenomenon, all of them unwritten. But the key to the real problem was to recognize that long established self-perceptions require time and opportunity for new experiences to effect change. Congruence between self-image and the outside world's view of us takes time to develop. No instant results could be available here.

Established self-perceptions are habits of thought. The lovely young lady had developed the emotional habit of seeing herself as ugly. She had believed something that became untrue. But beliefs don't shake easily. She had thought of herself in unattractive ways for so many years that it was hard to stop. To react to herself as a beautiful person was to feel like a liar. She knew that delight should be the new and proper response to herself, but habit dictated that she respond with self-depreciation. The conflict of competing emotions occasionally made her think that it was easier just to be unattractive. Her mind was so programmed to see herself as unacceptable that every automatic mental response was geared accordingly. But slowly she began to believe the new truth and to enjoy its blessings. Several years later she surprised me at a conference I was addressing. Still single, but very attractive, she now feared people no longer. Her abilities had brought her much success and joy.

In the previous chapter we defined agape love as the unmerited favor of God, given to all men. This love is unceasing, unchanging, unearned. It never stops even though man does not respond in kind. The example of the young woman trying to accept herself with a new and wonderful appearance is like our experience when we confront the work of God for us. In order to accept it and experience agape love, we must shed habits of long standing. The deeply ingrained tendency to see ourselves as acceptable only if we perform well by human standards must alter.

Only if we were reasonably attractive to God would we be accepted, we think, but the truth of the matter is that God loves us and calls us just, righteous, whole people whether or not we have attained that status with our fellow man. The question is: What perceptions shall I allow to

dominate my mental experience? Shall I accept myself as the forgiven object of unmerited love? Or shall I perceive myself in the tired old way, as working constantly to make myself acceptable in some human system of approval?

God's approval is a free gift. Your challenge is to believe it and let it soak in until all vestiges of guilt, inferiority, and unhappiness have disappeared. Adjust to the real truth about yourself, and let human assessments become clearly secondary. You have a personal, vital choice to make in the matter!

5 Validating Oneself as an Adequate Person

The adult seeks much of his adequacy through occupational achievements. I once knew a chiropractor who was so concerned about his image as an adequate person that he insisted his children address him as "Doctor."

Successful employment brings an adult prestige, status and income. These results entitle him to purchase certain symbols of success: the classic car, the ultra-modern home and the diet guaranteed to produce an acid stomach.

The usual route to these goals is to establish oneself in a line of work and climb step by step to higher levels of attainment. This is expressly true if formal training leading to a professional career is involved. With continued progress, the achiever receives the prized titles, salaries and plush, thick office carpets that label him a superior person.

In my field of college teaching, specific designations mark our progress. If we perform adequately, or at least get old enough, we reap the rewards of more distinguished ranks and titles. Others accord us a little more deference when we are labeled "Professor" rather than "Assistant Professor." Our vanity inflates, and we can safely assume airs of adequacy.

About May of each year, faculty tension mounts as each person awaits word from the president concerning possible advancement. Sometimes tears are shed when the proclamation arrives declaring success or failure to obtain new status. The threat of failure to obtain the higher ranks devastates some who have chosen rank designation as the criterion of adequacy. Bitterness hounds the footsteps of the critically disappointed. But for the more fortunate, the self-perceived image is enhanced, and life looks rosier. Fed enough of these psychological vitamins, we think we are truly Dr. Somebody.

A graduate professor asked a class I attended a provocative question that reveals the significance of achievement as a symbol and measure of adequacy. "If you could interview someone, but could ask only one question and by its answer determine the maximum amount of information about the individual, what would you ask?" We pondered his query for a time, and then because of the nature of the subject under study, we found the obvious reply. It was, "What do you do for a living?"

The response to this question reveals nearly all the important personal characteristics that relate to achievement. It indicates or suggests the amount and kind of education the person has received. In turn, the level of schooling reveals a clue to the individual's general knowledge and intelligence.

Further, we find that people move toward occupations that fit their self-images as closely as possible. Thus by learning what they do for a living, we obtain an insight into how they see themselves. Jobs become personal theaters where we play our roles before the public. If we are dominant and aggressive, we seek jobs in which we can enact these characteristics. If we are retiring or shy, we choose work that shields us from extensive public view. If we are unable to find reasonable harmony between our self-images and our jobs, one or the other will change. Usually it is the job, for a great change in one's perceived self in a short period of time is unlikely. Employment that is not self-assuring and enhancing is soon abandoned.

The job we hold also places us in a certain level of socioeconomic status. We therefore move in a social class that gives us further designation. Roles are implicit in the various classes and levels of social status, and members tend to act accordingly. Thus a man's job tells us something about the typical mode of public behavior of the individual. A doctor cannot conduct himself publicly in the same way as a labor organizer, nor a public official in the same way as a bartender. So, by his employment a person receives the rewards of society, finding both a role and an identification for himself.

The need for achievement is not confined merely to adult experience, but is shared by the very young as well. Even the tiny tot shows evidence of the need to achieve, to master his world. "Look at me, look at me!" shouts the four-year-old as he ties his shoes for the first time. Having mastered a task earlier than most children, he wants to be recognized as an adequate person as a result.

Tiny infants enjoy manipulating some element of their crib-encaged worlds. Research indicates that we have probably underestimated the learning potential that exists in the very young. Professor Jerome Kagan, of Harvard University, has said, "Babies are novelty-digesting machines that devour change." His studies of the intellectual development of the very young indicate a mastery of more advanced and complex information than we had thought possible. Given the opportunity to manipulate objects and toys in a stimulating environment, they pursue mental experience vigorously and seek the satisfaction it brings.

The school pupil finds his adequacy interpreted very directly to him by his achievements. Symbolized by grades from teachers, school records have blessed or plagued millions of people. Those who succeed are honored, see their names published in the paper, and enjoy the plaudits of school officials as well as of the community. In contrast, those who are labeled failures can find academic life a harsh, bitter experience. A significant number of pupils dubbed inadequate fail because of the imposition of impossible standards. Slow and unable to learn quickly, they receive the disapproval of a massive and socially powerful organization. It may be no fault of their own, but the resulting poor self-image can be a handicap for life. Forced to accept failure, they may turn to other means of determining adequacy. Physical prowess, antisocial behavior, or violence may be their method of retaliation. Much deviant behavior derives from a forced reduction in personal adequacy.

The need to achieve adequacy continues into old age. Observe the professor, who at the end of his career, turns to writing a significant text or takes up an entirely new avocation. Recently, at the time of his retirement, a professor of elementary education launched himself into the field of botany. A beginner with a very late start, he published two stimulating books for gardeners who wanted to understand the scientific aspects of their hobby. As a result, he received more acclaim for his botanical gardening than for his success as a university teacher.

Another professor, whose works I have sampled, was reported to have been working on nine texts at the time of his death. The motive to achieve continues with us until we die.

So we are propelled to achieve. But a most important question arises. What is the true measure of adequacy?

Is it really achievement? or learning? or status? Or are these standard contrivances of fumbling humans? Maybe there is something more valid by which we ought to measure man. I marvel that people struggle all their lives to produce some sense of self-worth and never ask whether the standards by which they judge their worth are valid. My thinking was focused sharply on this matter on one particularly poignant occasion.

I had been privileged to join a group of learned men in a research organization that studied the concerns of public education. These men brought to bear the finest critical minds and the most recent research techniques. It did not take long for me to discover that I was least among the members of this astute body. I learned far more than I contributed. Frequently, I doubted the worth of my contributions to sessions where my talents were lost in the plethora of sharpened skills of my colleagues.

As time went by, a pecking order developed in this little society. This was not an unusual happening; it occurs wherever people join together for any productive task. The people of demonstrable aptitude almost always emerge as the leaders. It is natural for society to rank persons in the order of their worth to the group. So it was with us. The usual sociological phenomenon was evident.

The chairman of our group turned out to be a man of outstanding qualities. He was the president of a corporation engaged in psychological research. As a sideline, he operated an unusually successful school for emotionally disturbed children. He had frequently been a leader in national research organizations. I liked him for his ability to get the best from each of us. It gave us a sense of usefulness and renewed our zest for the work. And I needed that! His philosophical approach to our task was refreshing to us as we dealt with tedious technical problems. He continually observed the possible consequences of our work and kept us sensitive to its meaningfulness.

61

One Thursday morning as we waited for the chairman's arrival, I began to analyze why I thought so highly of him. Clearly he exceeded others in talent and capacity. Perhaps this man was a model one might well emulate. Suddenly my thinking was interrupted. The vice-chairman bluntly opened the session. "The chairman will not be present today," he said. "Last night Charlie put a .38 revolver to his head and blew his brains out."

We sat stunned for a long moment, not daring to venture a word for fear all of us would lose our equilibrium.

As nearly as we could ascertain, Charlie made a conscious decision to end his existence without the precipitating causes that sometimes bring men to this terrible act. He had simply decided that the struggle to live, to be adequate, to amount to something was not worth it. But by most human standards, he "had it made."

Stunned as we were, a second shock wave proved to be even more unnerving. All of us suddenly realized that the goals we sought, our reasons for living, were very much the same as his. If Charlie's reasoning was correct, what was to prevent others of us from reaching the same conclusion about life?

Charlie had apparently decided that achievement as a standard for adequacy was an empty promise. He was educated, wealthy, successful, fulfilled, loved—by human terms of measurement, that is. But the results were not good enough! Dissatisfaction and meaninglessness in life still gnawed deeply at his soul. He had asked supreme questions: What is my reason for existence? How shall I truly determine my worth? Is achievement the key to adequacy? But he had found no satisfactory answers.

At the end of my undergraduate studies, a philosophy professor offered our class this parting thought: "Beware of what you want the most; you may get it." He was simply telling us, "By the time you have spent your life pursuing an objective, it may have lost its savor. Your goals may not have been valuable enough for you to invest in them a lifetime of work and hope. The standard that measures your adequacy and your reason for existence may have gone out of style, or crumbled beneath a weight of research, or tumbled before some social movement. Or like Charlie, you may find life empty even when you possess all the symbols of fulfillment. So how will you determine your adequacy? How will you validate your efforts? What criterion will you choose to measure the outcomes of life?"

It is a key thesis of this book that any *human* standard of adequacy is faulty and questionable. It is inevitably subject to human error. It is always limited to the maximum power of human perception. Instead, a definition of adequacy must be found that exceeds these limits; one that avoids the flaws of man's derived values and limited perceptions. The determination of how man attains true adequacy and of what constitutes a valid reason for existence must rest on eternal verities. Man needs a *revelation* of adequacy, for thus far, human history is poor testimony to mankind's ability either to be adequate or to set standards for adequacy. Time is running out.

One reason for doubting purely human standards of adequacy, particularly the criterion of achievement, is that the competition is unfair. Having spent many hours struggling with the problems of handicapped children, I appreciate the reality of this inequality. Is it fair that some people should be tragically handicapped in the struggle to attain fulfillment through achievement? A number of individuals have problems so great that they become a burden rather than a blessing to society. Their deficiencies preclude any recognized opportunity to achieve. The result is discouragement and a sense of uselessness.

Perhaps the problem of mental deficiency is the one that hurts the most. I vividly recall my experience explaining to two status-conscious parents that their newborn baby

63

was hopelessly retarded. Both parents were highly educated. Both were teachers in well-known colleges. The mother had obtained the finest prenatal care. The baby was born in one of the most up-to-date children's hospital in the world—it served as a training school in pediatrics for a large university medical school. What better place to get started in life?

When the baby was born, it was immediately apparent that he suffered from Down's syndrome—mongolism. The etiology is partly known; apparently a genetic malfunction causes the child to inherit an extra chromosome. The pediatrician who made the diagnosis was one of the world's leading researchers in the field of mental retardation. He was also a skilled person in handling the emotions of people, a fact that helped only a little as we explained the facts to the parents of the child.

At first the mother and father acted as if they were completely in control of the experience. The husband calmly made arrangements to have the child placed in an institution. Rejecting our advice, they would not take him home with them. But the cool control slowly turned to deep bitterness and hate. Each day they became more enraged at the hospital, at the doctor, at me, at life, at God! What sense did it make to allow a retarded child to be born to them—intelligent, educated people whose reputations could only suffer by having a stupid kid around?

The parents placed their child in the institution, and for a time it appeared that they had gained some relief. But it was not so. In sixty days, the couple instituted court proceedings to recover custody of the child, now living in a public institution as a ward of the state. The guilt of the mother in rejecting the child precipitated the action. She had rejected her own offspring and could not bear the hurt.

The parents had two serious problems. Seeking adequacy

64

through status and academic achievement, they felt unable to tolerate the questions that would be raised by the presence of a retarded child. Surely a retarded youngster would cast aspersions on their intellectual superiority! They were painfully torn between the need to maintain status and the need to reduce guilt. But overwhelmed by the guilt of rejecting the child in an institution, they had him returned to their home.

Their mode of child rearing was pitiful. Afraid to show him to the world, they hid him at home during his early years. Few people knew that they had had a retarded child, whom they were now denying any chance for personal or social development. Bitterness and hostility dominated the parents' lives. Repeatedly they asked, "Why is life so unfair to us and to this child?"

It is clear that if adequacy comes chiefly through achievement, then the present standard is unfair. Since so many can't measure up, this criterion becomes an oppressive goad. Whole segments of our society have experienced the injustice of some handicap. Large portions of the elementary school population in most cities are labeled "disadvantaged," or "unfairly handicapped," in their efforts to find adequacy through achievement.

Whatever standard is in vogue seems to dictate who is to be adequate or perhaps elite. A notable shift in the definition of adequacy took hold of our public schools a few years ago. With the great achievement of the Soviet Union in launching the first space satellite, American schools received a bruising from every possible critic. "Our schools are not turning out adequate students!" was the cry. "We must have tougher requirements!"

Prior to this time, in the view of the students, the adequate youngster was not necessarily an academic. Instead, he was a combination of several elements. He was required to be an early maturing male or an average-to-early matur-

ing female. Physical attractiveness was an important factor in acceptance. Brilliance was revered, but studiousness was not. Grades that were too high could make one suspect. The key to acceptance was athletic prowess. Decorated with letters, sweaters, pins and patches, the athlete was king! Students with this combination of characteristics were most often chosen by their peers to positions of leadership. They obtained the most significant status symbols. In short, they received the label "adequate." They suffered less social stress, and generally enjoyed themselves.

But times changed. Public emphasis shifted to rewarding academic ability. The National Defense Act became law. Scholarships grew in number and were awarded most often to students specializing in science and mathematics. Some schools began to award letters and sweaters to students for academic achievement as well as athletic competence. So now who is adequate? Who now has the advantage of achieving easily a self-image of importance? Suddenly, the egghead found himself in public favor and could hardly believe it.

Because of rising standards for academic competence, some schools experienced an increased drop-out rate. Students found it easier to leave than to face higher probabilities of failure. Other schools found the public less willing to finance the usual sports programs together with other activities.

In short, while we are searching for adequacy, the standards may alter. In times of rapid social change, these standards shift much more quickly. The advantages may go to some other class of persons, so why hunt for an elusive criterion? Further, the achievement criterion always dictates inadequacy for some!

High-school and college-age young people go through periods of intense self-assessment. Questions about the validity of human experience rise forcefully in their minds. These young people begin to look at the standards held for validating themselves and ask a lot of troublesome questions. Perhaps the fatiguing nature of introspection turns them from self-assessment to judgments of the standards they are expected to uphold.

The typical youngster is taking a long look at what the world holds as standards of adequacy. He wonders if there is an alternative to the standard of educational or occupational achievement which gives advantages to some and dictates failure to others, especially when a great increase in general technical knowledge is required of everyone. With every new development, the minimum standard rises a little.

The young person views many different adult models of achievement. He sees individuals of the Charlie-type we mentioned earlier—capable, effective, achieving, but feeling worthless enough to end it all. Then he stumbles on a simple, forthright, sensitive human being who has mastered little of the economic world but who retains a glow for life that defies explanation. In college he encounters the studious philosopher who has no better answer to life's problems than some pushy gadget salesman. Supposedly, the scholar of the metaphysical world would come up with better answers than the peddler, but he does not. Sometimes his answers seem worse. I recall, somewhat dimly now, a poll of professors of philosophy. The results indicated that only a small percentage had committed themselves to a particular philosophy of life. That is scarcely a remarkable symptom of certainty, is it?

Those who obtain the common goals of status, wealth, or educational achievement fare no better than the philosophers. They come to the end of their experiences offering no better judgments than anyone else. The dominant remembrances of the successful are as often those of frustration, threat of loss, and fears accumulated from high risks taken, as those of the joys of self-fulfillment. The successful people of our time are not the glowing examples of life lived for its intrinsic value or meaningfulness.

Why can't human beings create a definition of adequacy, and having achieved it, be assured that life will be meaningful and valid? This question especially spoofs the youngster who decides to become a fully educated humanitarian. He often turns from the usual definition of achievement to a stereotyped life of nonachieving humanitarianism. He may choose to live simply, dress shabbily, accumulate little of life's junk, and do his own thing. In time he accomplishes important tasks. He relieves suffering, improves the educational level of the poor, opens men's eyes to the beauties of nature and themselves. He reflects that he has not contributed to war, violence, or hunger. "What nobler goal could I pursue?" he questions in rationalized thought. "Surely becoming a humanitarian develops intrinsic qualities of adequacy within me."

No one seriously doubts the need for humanitarian efforts. We cannot live long without them. But the fact remains that people who choose humanitarian pursuits do not experience a great deal more fulfillment or sense of adequacy than do others. I have observed many colleagues who chose higher education as a profession in some faint hope that the humanitarian aspects of the occupation would make them become adequate people. This did not happen. Perhaps I could make the same judgment about those who enter the clergy.

Both those who choose achievement as a means to adequacy and those who regard traditional achievement as an obstacle to adequacy conclude their experiences with doubts about their own value. Once a physics professor remarked to me, "What good is it? All I can say is that maybe I didn't hurt anyone as much as if I had done something else!"

My personal conclusion is that the nature of the occupation one chooses is a secondary factor, rather than a primary factor, in our perceptions of our adequacy. While I find it necessary to rule out such occupations as working for breweries, gambling syndicates, or pornography publishers, I cannot look to my occupational choice as a primary determinant of adequacy. The fact that most people *do* estimate their adequacy in terms of their occupations and their achievements does not alter this conclusion.

Occupational choice and satisfaction grow out of a sense of adequacy, not the other way around. An adequate person chooses a job or profession that allows him to enact the sense of adequacy and fulfillment that he already has. While his work may reinforce his sense of adequacy, it is not the primary factor in determining it. This is why two people can enter the same occupational field and have entirely different experiences. One enters the job looking for something he does not have. He has fond hopes that he can live in the sparkle of his title and see himself as Mr. Important. The other man starts with an assumption of adequacy and proceeds to live out an adequate self-life in his world of work. Sometimes the work is reinforcing, sometimes he keeps at it in spite of the feedback he gets. But his self-perception is based primarily on factors other than his achievements. His achievements are by-products of a fulfilled life.

Adequacy, therefore, is *cause* rather than *effect*. Adequacy leads to fulfilled humanitarian experience. It stimulates noble achievement. While achievement may in time reinforce one's sense of adequacy, it is not the chief stimulus. Something more than need for mastery or achievement, something other than success, calls us to fulfilled lives.

Surely the time comes when every farmer must lay down his hoe and call it a day. Achievement ends for us all. Most of us see it terminate before life is over. If our sense of adequacy has depended upon achievements, any curtailment of opportunity can be sheer misery. Many retirements have been cut short by the deaths of persons who lost hold of the means to bolster self-perceptions. But if adequacy was the cause rather than the effect of achievement, how different those days are! The loss of achievement may be painful, but adequacy remains.

If adequacy is cause rather than effect, it suggests a hypothesis about motivation. Adequacy is a stronger motivation to achievement than achievement is to adequacy. The analogy of motivation in guilt reduction supports this idea for it may be argued that guilt and a lack of adequacy are almost synonymous. Guilt motivates a man to seek relief long enough to reduce his stress. When he obtains relief, he stops. Adequacy, on the other hand, is an unceasing stimulus to achievement. Motivation continues because there are always endless worlds yet to conquer. When achievement reinforces an already present sense of adequacy, motivation increases, and it is not terminated by temporary guilt reduction. If you want to be an achiever, seek a basis other than achievement for your fulfillment.

With reasoning such as this I often ask students, "Are you an adequate student because you seek to avoid failure, or because you act out of a sense of achievement and fulfillment?" "Are your A's symptoms of your struggle with guilt, or are they the by-product of an adequate self?"

In lectures before numerous groups of people, I have challenged them to investigate the New Testament thoroughly and determine exactly what God thinks of them.

70

MAN AGAPE LOVE

I ask, "Does He regard you as adequate or not? What is God's view of you?" (See Romans 8:1,16,17.)

The writers of the Scriptures are careful to point out that when God looks at you in Jesus Christ, He sees you as a brother to His own Son. Because of the work of Christ, all the ugliness of humanity is set aside. God has absolutely no attitude of condemnation toward man. You are worth all of God's attention. If you were the only person in the whole world, it would be worth God's effort to make Himself known to you and to love you. He gives you freely the status and adequacy of an heir to the universe.

This is agape love, the unmerited, unconditional favor of God for man. We achieve our adequacy through this unceasing love. We do not *become* sufficient, approved, or adequate; rather we are *declared to be* such! When we believe this, we become achievers and humanitarians as an effect, a by-product of our newfound selves.

How can true adequacy be placed on us simply by pronouncement? Most of us find this difficult to accept. Certainly it would not accrue to us through purely human efforts. People might label us with many titles, but that would not in any way guarantee that we have changed. We are not now dealing with man, however; we are dealing

71

with God. All the conditions of relationship are different so that the usual rules for relationship do not apply. This relationship of love continues unceasingly. You can't lose it by goofing things up somewhere.

Most of us have spent our lives dealing in bartered relationships. We have exchanged good behavior for parental love. Or we have repaid hurt with hurt. We have earned the symbols of adequacy from this world through our achievements. All of these relationships have been mutually dependent. They have existed as long as both parties kept their agreements. We have become so accustomed to behaving in these terms that when conditions change, we hardly know how to act. We perpetually seek to pay for gifts thrust on us, or we give an eye for an eye and a tooth for a tooth.

Have you ever tried to give someone something freely, only to find yourself repaid in spite of all your efforts to the contrary? Some folks cannot get out of the rut of bartering every facet of relationship! One day I found myself in this predicament on a golf course. I had played badly through the early part of the match and lost all the balls I brought along. Seeing my plight, my opponent reached into his bag with two massive hands and came out with over a dozen high-quality balls. He dumped them on the ground by my clubs and simply said, "Take these."

"But I can't take all that!" I countered. "That's too much! Those pellets cost money!"

"Aren't you big enough to take something from a friend?" His voice was strident as he spoke. "Better pick them up or somebody else will get them." With mixed feelings of joy over my treasure of golf balls and humiliation because of my initial refusal, I quickly stuck the balls into my golf bag.

What really happened was this: I was attempting to barter a relationship that he intended me to enjoy on a totally free basis. I had resisted his love. But what hurt me most was the fact that this man had sought me out to get help with a definite problem he faced in his life. And he turned out to be the better man! By his gift, I was sure, he was not buying my help; he clearly wanted that free relationship that exists when both parties give themselves in agape love. He also wanted the gift of help from me as a free expression of love.

So frequently we deal with God on the same basis. We insist on bartering when He would give us His gifts freely. He offers us forgiveness, status, adequacy, direction in life. Instead of responding with thanks and love, we insist on earning the gift or trading something for it. We become so religious nobody can stand us. Or we refuse His gift and say that we do not deserve it. Or we become so aseptically moral that no needy human can touch us. We forget so quickly that Jesus was the one who took care of any shortage of payment we owe, or any bartering that had to be done. He gave Himself so that we could freely receive. You can be adequate. You can be guilt-free! Accept His love. Your doubts about the truth of the matter will vanish when you do. He will put His spirit within you, and honest joy will surprise you.

When a person has accepted adequacy as a gift, he immediately perceives a new standard for achievement. No longer does the criterion of human performance apply, but rather the measure of faithfulness judges us. This is the fair standard, the one that stimulates everyone, frustrates no one, and is administered by the providential will of God.

What is required of a man is that he be found faithful, to paraphrase 1 Corinthians 4:2. He should perform to the limits of his ability in the tasks God gives him to do. He should be free from social pressures to conform to the world's standards of achievement—free to do the things he is truly able and motivated to do.

73

Adopting faithfulness as a criterion has a multiple impact on a person's life. If he has had an uphill struggle trying to amount to something, he experiences relief. By now, his tolerance for failure has probably been well tested, and his motivation may have seriously diminished. For him an impossible standard of human performance, which has dictated inadequacy for so many, has lost its punch. The sock of failure is gone. But now, with a new sense of interest and certainty, he can proceed again, knowing that God is his judge, not a human taskmaster. Doing appropriate tasks judged by more reasonable standards, he finds acceptance from the One who really matters.

For awhile, however, he is probably going to struggle with ambivalence—those bothersome, mixed emotions that slowly resolve themselves. Occasionally he may return to human standards that bring again a sense of failure, because everyone insists on their validity. But surely he can, in time, adjust his sights to measure himself by the sure criterion of faithfulness.

The ambivalence comes from the fact that he must reject long accepted values. And rejection isn't automatic or easy. These values hold on when he would be free of them. It's like trying to kick a stubborn habit. Now he reevaluates people who once stimulated his drive to produce beyond his means. As he sees the way in which they have unwittingly victimized him, he experiences occasional hostility toward those he once revered. He may be tempted from time to time to act out his feelings, but hurting his unthinking friends has no value either. Instead, the relaxation that comes from shedding impossible goals will refresh his mind and relieve his anxiety about his work.

To the person graced with many human capacities, the standard of faithfulness is not easy. He must reckon with new realities and face tough demands. Those performances he accomplished with little effort, but which the community rewarded handsomely, lose much of their luster. The ego fattened by continuous, easily obtained rewards gets an unexpected jolt. The false self-image constructed over the years experiences a humbling discovery. The person gains a new perspective. He sees that more is required than ever before.

Ambivalence again becomes a bit of a problem. The temptation to relax and settle for human judgments that inflate the psyche is hard to resist. But there is something so therapeutic about reality that in time the increased requirement of faithfulness for the well endowed is a refreshing, redemptive experience. One becomes a lover of the truth, even the truth about oneself.

Faithfulness taps the limits of us all. Rather than facing the human standard, which is easy for some and difficult for others, we all are measured by the degree to which we use our God-given capacities. Another impact of the faithfulness criterion is that, freed from human standards, we can pursue endeavors that are also free from human systems of value and reward. We can pursue some improbable missions, attempting creative enterprises because failure no longer looms so deadly as before. We are ready to enjoy pursuits that others would undertake with anxiety, fearing failure.

For example, one may find himself able to leave a promising career in the middle of his best years and do something very unlikely but infinitely useful. I know a number of doctors, teachers, architects, agricultural specialists who left the usual human track of progress and gave themselves away in service to God and man. Traveling to some faraway chunk of foreign soil, they found themselves enriched by faithful living. No longer enslaved by their own success, they became free, faithful men.

The greatest human experience occurs when one can assess oneself both as the object of supreme love and as one who has been faithful in expending all his talents in faithful, agape service to God and man.

75

While doing psychological work in a large high school, I became acquainted with a nineteen-year-old junior—rather ancient for the third year of high school. The problem was that he had failed U.S. History three times, as well as several other subjects, and just couldn't get out of the place. History was always taught by the same teacher, a hard-nosed fellow who believed in being academically tough. Thanks to this generous supplier of F grades, my friend was at an impasse.

The young man suffered from handicaps that reduced his verbal intelligence significantly, though his other abilities seemed intact. His birth had been most difficult, and he had suffered serious brain damage and facial disfigurement. The usual pattern in such cases is for the handicapped person to reject those who administer failure while venting hostility fully. He often develops an angry, brooding tendency that begins to dominate most of his human relationships. Life becomes a series of unfortunate encounters and further failures.

But this boy had a special kind of motivation. Knowing his limits, he maintained his motivation by recognizing that he need not dread failure so long as he performed to the limits of his ability. He judged himself by the standard of faithfulness in using the talents he had, not by the teacher's inclination to impose an impossible standard.

As we talked, he showed an assurance about his self-esteem that was spiritually based. He was convinced that he had been the recipient of God's grace and that all other assessment factors were secondary. Having known this kind of fulfillment, he insisted on finishing high school so that he could be of maximum use to God and man. His diploma would be a means to help him give himself away.

We were able to make appropriate adjustments in the boy's high-school program and finally got him through history with a passable grade. In due time he graduated and has since done construction work for missionaries in another country. If he had judged himself by the usual standards, I have no doubt that the outcome would have been very different.

6 The Need for Authentic Living

Eric Berne's book, *Games People Play,** has captured the attention of thousands of people. Presumably it bears this title because it describes how people relate to each other in non-authentic ways. I recommend it because of the many useful insights it brings. Describing many elaborately contrived modes of behavior, it tells how we learn to transact our business with each other while concealing feelings.

In non-authentic living, there is a behavioral recipe to follow in nearly every social situation. If we know the place where we are going to be and the kind of people who will be there, our behavior can be predicted fairly well. We will unconsciously follow the behavioral recipe that fits the situation.

The roles we play may serve useful functions. Our assumption of roles solves certain problems. It gives others a feeling of certainty about us. When we abide by the social rules, we become predictable people. We are less likely to pull any dramatic surprises. As a result others

*Eric Berne. *Games People Play: The Psychology of Human Relationships* (New York: Grove Press. 1964).

are more comfortable in our presence and we feel more secure. Our minds are relatively free to deal with whatever subject or problem comes up. We are not preoccupied with curiosity or uncomfortableness about one another's actions. So we can temper our actions with love. Therefore, complete honesty or authenticity is not always the best course to follow.

For my own fun one day I taught a college class dressed in a bright orange shirt, yellow alpaca sweater, olive green slacks, red socks, and black-and-white golf shoes. I lectured on the theory of correlation statistics to a graduate seminar, but needless to say, nobody heard a word I said or comprehended any theory. Abstract information on a boring subject produced little interest when the person divulging it looked as though he had fallen into a paint mixer. The glaring colors were completely distracting, for they were inconsistent with the role of the typical professor. So everyone was thrown a little off balance.

My purpose for this stunt was twofold; first, I had a college golf match to supervise after class and, then, I just felt like stepping out of role for a brief time. I had been professorial long enough. Professors get a bit stuffy and become so predictable that too much of the time they interest nobody.

I am reminded of a colleague who dressed almost the same way every day for years. He always wore a blue tweed suit with vest and with his watch chain draped across his paunch. And he never knew what time it was. Nobody ever saw him dressed any other way or ever caught him looking at his watch. I suspect that if I stopped at his home and found him mowing the lawn or carrying out the garbage, he would be wearing a blue tweed suit with watch in place, wondering what time it was.

This man had completely absorbed the professorial role. He was a professor everywhere. When he went to buy garden fertilizer, you could be sure he was a professor, not a gardener. His dress, his manner, his attitude always tipped you off to the fact that he could see himself in no other way. He had been trapped inflexibly in a role and image.

Youngsters learn to play roles early. Boys are taught to play the rough role. Strong boys don't cry, only the sissy ones do. Masculine little men achieve their place in the sun by physical superiority over others. It's all part of the game. Then when they become adults they can't understand why their wives cry over so many things. The wife in turn thinks her husband is a cold, hard, unsympathetic stoic who fails to appreciate her problems.

One professor I knew had been a dean in a large college. When a new president was appointed to the school, he promptly demoted my acquaintance. But the role of dean was so ingrained that he couldn't stop deaning! In department meetings he would "take over" as the dominant personality. He expected his ideas to be received uncritically by his peers. Constantly referring to himself as the senior member of the group, he expected to enjoy status and privilege he was no longer entitled to. As a result, he was an obstacle to solving problems in the department. Furthermore, his feelings were always getting hurt, and he couldn't figure out why.

While playing predictable roles gives us certainty about each other, it can stereotype the uniqueness right out of us. Our freedom to act spontaneously and honestly gets lost. Further, we force ourselves into molds that often fit us uncomfortably in an attempt to absolve conflict between the mold and our true selves. More and more of our behavior becomes patterned uncomfortably after some expected role. To reduce conscious stress, we subdue our sensitivities and our true feelings.

If we are insecure ourselves, or those around us are especially timid, we feel a great deal of pressure to play roles. Any variance in the behavior of others creates questions about how we should behave. We in turn become less predictable and therefore more threatening. Violating expected roles can be very upsetting to shaky people, so we apply pressure to keep us safe either from ourselves or from others.

After playing games for long periods of time, we lose our uniqueness, our authenticity. We become insensitive to our own feelings. When others deal with us, they deal with a person playing a role, not the real person. The difference between our role and who we really are can sometimes become so wide that an observer might think we had a split personality.

Several years ago I counseled with a minister who had denied his feelings through role playing. He was a man with a long history of personal problems and had sought the ministerial role to cover his faults and hurts. As long as he could manifest the appearance of sanctimony, he seemed to get by, for it drove his conflicts underground. In time, however, he developed an illicit attachment for a woman in another city. He was shocked by his own feelings and behavior, but could not discontinue the relationship.

The whole sordid mess eventually came into the open and the congregation he served responded valiantly. Instead of pronouncing judgment and acting punitively, they chose a better way. He had expected that they would treat him as an outcast and strip him of his job. Instead, they dealt with him as a man in great need, and gave assurance and support to his wife who had been sent reeling by the experience. For the first time he began dealing with his own life in authentic terms and getting honest help.

The concealing of his true self in acceptable roles ended. The tension broke. Had he been allowed to deal with his hurts in earlier years, he might never have received this crisis, but as a youngster he had been taught to play always the role of a good boy. Just play the role of a model child.

Never admit that anything bothers you and it won't. Put the lid on troubled feelings. Deny any difficult emotional experience. Always protect your image.

After working in other employment for several years while undergoing counseling and therapy, he returned to the ministry, a healed man with many talents to use productively. With a new sense of freedom, he is ministering more capably than ever before.

The pressure to assume roles can sometimes mount past our ability to endure. The pressure comes frequently from the threat of having to pay a high price for breaking out of a confining role.

A young woman I knew belonged to a certain religious sect that was identified by unusual clothes. Appearing old-fashioned, she suffered under the taunts of her classmates in school. Courses in sewing and home economics were nearly unbearable. She could not work on anything her peers regarded as attractive, and she was forbidden by her parents to use the sewing machines provided at school.

Other problems attended her, too. Physically, her mother was marked by scars caused by a serious accident. She rejected her own appearance and reinforced negative attitudes toward physical appearance in her daughter. Unwittingly she instructed her daughter in the roles of self-rejection and self-deprecation.

Searching for a way to change her low self-estimates, she provoked long theological arguments with her parents. These attacks were unconsciously designed to test the most sensitive and protected areas of the parents' life—a common tactic of troubled youngsters.

Mother made it abundantly clear that rejecting her theology was unforgivable. Furthermore, any challenge to the dress codes of her group was theological rejection. If the daughter insisted on stepping out of the religious role and out from under her mother's projected unhappiness, she was rejecting God. The role of conformity was being rein-forced by ultimate weapons: God, family and mother's neurosis.

The result was sad. The girl buckled, absorbing intense guilt and dropped out of school. She was labeled unworthy, and her needs were ignored. Her feelings were completely sacrificed at the altar of mother's need for self-protection. Deeply depressed, she never married or assumed any self-support. She remains totally dependent on her parents even now in their old age.

Suppose that the authentic problem had been faced. If the mother had been given support in facing her own problem of appearance, might the daughter's happiness have been salvaged? If the taunts of classmates had been recognized and faced as a threat, would the youngster have been unconsciously prompted to attack the theological premises of the family and church? Would she have used the theological question to screen her real needs? If the girl could have realistically looked at the mother's projected self-deprecation, would she have absorbed so much guilt? Would she then have had to choose the role of dependency for life to resolve her guilt?

Situations like this, that need honest review and authentic self-presentation, come up in every home at some time or other, although often on a smaller scale. Every home impresses on its children some semblance of required role. The external symptoms may not include rigidly defined dress standards, but nevertheless the role characteristics are there. I can see some of this in my own family as well.

My children's parents are educated well beyond the usual limits. Mother and father have five college degrees between them. The four grandparents have seven degrees. What are the chances that my kids can play any role other than that of children of an overeducated family?

Fortunately, they are doing well in school, and this may

relieve the pressure somewhat. The role may in fact become completely normal and comfortable. But if it does not, I hope that we will have insight and grace enough to recognize the fact and deal authentically with it.

Our culture has developed many professionally described roles. Perhaps the best example of this is conveyed by the medical profession. Careful training in what is known as bedside manner and rigid professional ethics establish the norm for a doctor's behavior.

Suppose your doctor dealt with you authentically on all occasions. When you call him at 2 A.M. to tell him your left big toe hurts, how would he respond? Surely it would be unauthentic of you to make such a call at this hour, but let's be hypothetical. Your friendly purveyor of the healing arts, if acting authentically, would probably order you off the phone so he could get some sleep. But he doesn't respond this way. Instead, he is polite so that when a real crisis arises you won't hesitate to call.

The doctor's assumed role protects him in a number of ways. Since he constantly deals with stress and pain, his own tension could mount to unbelievable heights if he were unable to mask his true feelings. His unauthentic manner protects both you and him. Some shielding is necessary.

But the problem arises when we deal with others *all the time* from behind masks. Then people never know how we really feel. Nor can they tell us how they really feel. We mutually prod each other to play a role or to wear a mask, but we never tell it like it is. In time we are dulled into insensitivity and into predetermined, uncomfortable behavior. Our relationships deteriorate, and we fail to reach each other when we need genuine help.

The temptation to be less than authentic exists in the field of professional counseling as well. Like any other professional, we are tempted to mask many feelings because we know our attitudes are not always helpful. One particular morning stimulated me to hide securely behind a professional mask. I had scheduled a series of appointments to discuss problems of mental handicap with several parents of retarded children. Facing the realities of this difficult problem with parents occasionally is hard enough for a counselor, but struggling through six such cases in one morning was a serious tactical error.

The first parent arrived—dirty, unkempt, foulmouthed and ignorant. My best professional efforts to explain the problem produced only more stress. The parent rejected the problem completely and leveled a barrage of blame at the school system. I suppressed the urge to return in kind and waited for the next appointment.

The second mother arrived—dirty, unkempt, foulmouthed, ignorant and bad smelling. I was licked before I started. Retreating behind my wall of professional tactics, I took a very cool approach. I reflected the mother's feelings mechanically without stimulating any emotion in myself. I also held my breath to avoid the aroma drifting across the desk. My questions were suave. My conclusions were guarded with educational tentativeness. My recommendations were garnished with indefinite psychological gobbledygook. But I didn't get upset. Surely I could get along until a more acceptable client arrived for the next interview. Then I could resume being comfortable. But such was not the case.

Mother number three arrived. She was dirty, unkempt, foulmouthed, ignorant, bad smelling and extremely obese. I prayed for an emergency to call me out of the office. Maybe a teacher somewhere could choose this moment to crack up, and I could be called from my office to a distant school to render advice. No luck; no phone calls.

We were a few sentences into our conversation when this mother sensed I needed some help, too. She diverted from the subject and told me how much I had helped the lady who had just left. I was shocked. How could it be? I was sure I had garbled the whole previous interview and betrayed my frustration. But no, I had been lucky! She must have needed my cool approach.

The woman now sitting across the desk from me was perceptive. She sensed that I was masking something, and it was not helping her need, either. She was right, and I confessed my efforts to deny my own emotions. I admitted that I resisted dealing with people I did not like. The remainder of our conference looked past appearances and hindering feelings, and we were able to develop some solid understandings of the problems she faced.

Looking past appearances is the key to authenticity. It is the only way to stay helpfully vulnerable to people. Man looks at appearances, but God looks at the heart. A paraphrase of 1 Samuel 16:7 was turning over in my mind.

As mothers number four, five and six came through my office that morning, all mathematical probabilities failed. The parents were all the kind of people I was least prepared to deal with that day. But a simple statement by one of them had exposed my reluctant attitudes for what they were. As a result, I was prompted to return to more basic honesty. It was one of the toughest mornings I have ever had. It would have been easier for me to have kept on the mask and played the role of cool professional. But I had been stripped of my facade and I became a little more useful and a lot more tired as a result.

Love and authenticity are inseparable partners in our emotional lives. The security engendered by love allows us to take off our masks and lower the defenses that shut us off from the needs of others and from sensitivity to ourselves. Love allows us to look past the appearances that once protected us because they acted as barriers to reaching others. So love abolishes the mask that distorts perceptions.

The need for authentic living is a challenge to receive agape love and to become honest, sensitive people. And the result is a life rich in experience and full of meaning.

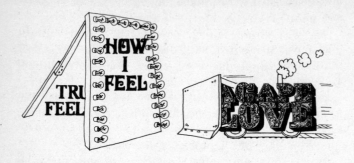

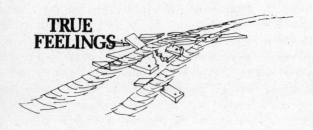

Living past appearances, under the dominating influence of God's love, allows us to enjoy our successes as well. No need to hide them as do some people who are more embarrassed by their achievements than their failures. To admit that one is successful is to risk denying experience again. It has become so popular to be self-effacing and falsely humble that some people can hardly perceive success. But if one has truly achieved, it is just as deceptive to deny success as it is to deny unacceptable feelings or actions.

I recall from my high school days a lad who had artistic ability in sculpting. His works were unusual and creative. But he was different. He matured late and suffered from a lack of physical abilities. Berated by his peers, he settled into social silence. He protected himself by playing the role of a nobody.

But the trouble was that he hid his genuine talents. In a fit of anger over the treatment by his peers, he smashed every object he had made. He rejected even the minimum symptoms of success.

In his senior year, a sensitive teacher encouraged him to return to his hobby. She guarded his feelings carefully, not letting anyone know he was back at work again. With her encouragement he produced a small statue that was displayed at the state fair. It won him immediate acclaim. His name was in the paper, and photos of his work were displayed. But it was more than he or his classmates could bear, for it shattered his facade of being a nobody.

When the news broke, several bullies hoisted him to their shoulders and paraded him around the campus. Shouting derogatory names and taunting him, they finished by dropping him in the fishpond in front of the main building. So great was the pressure to deny legitimate successful experience, that the boy refused to be successful any more. It was safer being nothing than being an achiever.

But love produces certainty of self, because we are the objects of the greatest of all love. With certainty, we sense less need to deny our experiences. This is true whether the experience is success or failure. When the need to deny our identity is reduced, we are free to launch out upon the joys and difficulties of authentic living, the kind of living that puts us in touch with people in redemptive, wholesome ways.

Authenticity, or honesty in living, has certain characteristics that are sometimes helpful to know. Knowing them can stimulate us to growth. Here are the signs of the authentic personality.

1. Adequacy and identity result from his relationships with man and God. The agape love experience is the mode

of his personal conduct. Agape love has affirmed the person, and he has responded in belief and in emotion to this love. He has absorbed this love so that he is now secure, appearing emotionally self-supporting and autonomous.

2. He finds his own personal experience increasingly satisfying and trustworthy. He revels in the joy of his own mental awarenesses. He can trust his feelings and has an accurate sense of judgment concerning the meaning of his experiences.

3. He has a nondefensive attitude toward people. He spends little effort protecting his image, reputation and feelings. He is free of anxiety in dealing with others.

4. He consciously avoids the use of defense mechanisms in painful situations because defensiveness tends to bring distortion of self and others.

5. His security and identity, resulting from agape love, make him open toward people. He sees people as like himself, seeking to make the most sense and meaning of life. As such he shares a common humanity with them.

6. He willingly shares his feelings and attitudes with others. He is not threatened by any subject of discussion. He is not surprised by unusual personal experiences.

7. His understanding of people goes beyond appearances, symbols, images and stereotypes. He regards all behavior as problem solving. He seeks to understand the unique perceptions and dynamics of each person.

8. He avoids categorical judgments of people. Instead, he is mindful of the uniqueness of each person. He regards all people as candidates for genuine growth and the opportunity to receive supreme love.

9. He regards differences of opinion among people as the result of their different backgrounds, experiences and perceptions. Only exceptionally are differences the result of deliberate dishonesty.

10. He crosses the lines of group identity readily: he

is a truly cross-cultural person. Since he understands and appreciates uniqueness, his relationships transcend group stereotypes and definitions.

11. He refrains from imposing his own categories, doctrinal designations, stereotypes, or judgments upon others. Instead he seeks to apply agape love to the unique problems of each person.

12. He tries to remain vulnerable to the widest range of human problems. He sees the need to be open and tentative in his estimation of unusual problems and the people who bear them.

In contrast, let us make a list of the behavioral symptoms of the nonauthentic person.

1. He gains his identity from the image he can construct with his personal occupational achievements.

2. He has a restricted range of contacts with people. He relates most easily to those of similar class designation, stereotype, or group status.

3. Observing rather strict loyalties to his own group, he has a fairly high rejection rate of other people. He deals with those who bear different names, classes, or designations only on remote terms. He sees them as needing to change in order to be included in his fellowship.

4. His conversations deal only with "safe" subjects. He is conscious of the need to make a number of behaviors and topics taboo. He believes that the answers to most human problems are known and, therefore, that further debate is unnecessary.

5. He does not permit himself to experience a wide range of emotions. He regards vulnerability to feeling as a sign of weakness.

6. Since he has predetermined answers to all problems—answers that conform to the mores and taboos of his own group, his emotional growth is steadily toward becoming an authoritarian personality.

7. He perceives those who disagree with him as either

dishonest or unenlightened. They are not to be trusted fully until they deal within the categories he prescribes and come to the predetermined conclusions he dictates.

8. He utilizes defense mechanisms frequently. Defense is the first priority in time of difficulty, for it precludes examination of his attitudes and feelings.

9. He compensates for his imperviousness to people by identifying with a "star" who epitomizes his favorite stereotype. Instead of thinking through a problem, he follows his leader and adopts his approaches and solutions.

10. He lives "in front of himself." One must deal with his image or self-presentation, not the real man. He relates to another person only if his protection is guaranteed.

1 The Need to Be Expended

Dr. Paul Carlson, the martyred medical servant of the people of Congo, was a college classmate and friend of mine. We had studied together, traveled together and in general kept in contact with each other for some time before he went to Africa.

Answering the call of the United Nations to furnish desperately needed medical help at the time of Congo's independence and revolution, Paul dedicated himself to do the obviously loving thing. He went to Africa because he was prepared to alleviate the existing need. A godly compulsion to give all of himself characterized his life.

After a couple of years, Paul's work, and that of a medical student assistant, caught the attention of a leading magazine, and a major news feature and picture story was prepared for publication. But as he was assisting the suffering, the great uprising occurred. He was captured by Congolese rebels, the Simbas, who claimed he was a foreign agent. While he was held prisoner in Stanleyville, thousands of us prayed impatiently for his release. After all, the rebels were not known for humanitarian behavior. When he and other prisoners were not released, rescue operations began. Planes were sent in an attempt to return as many captives as possible to safety. When the planes landed, the prisoners broke for freedom. But Paul's life ended in a hail of machine-gun bullets.

Immediately the story and pictures of his work, and the message of the supreme love of God for man that motivated him, was flashed throughout the world. Of his life one television commentator said, "Paul asked only for the opportunity to give, and it cost him his life."

The motivation and inspiration of his work were not lost, however. Today a medical foundation in the Congo continues Paul's selfless giving. His brother assumed his place as a medical servant to needy people. A beautiful science and learning center was built on the campus of our alma mater in his memory. The story of his life, by his widow, has had wide circulation. Paul became an example to the world of fulfillment through loving expendability.

When a person has been assured of his adequacy and worthiness by the loving acts of God, as Paul Carlson was, this assurance begins to permeate his most basic emotional responses. Almost automatically, a desire to expend himself rises sharply and becomes a dominant theme in his life. He yearns to plunge into something totally consuming. He seeks a hill big enough to die on. His life goes on the block: he lets God direct and use it in the most strategic way possible. No longer preoccupied with himself, he is free to surrender himself for others. The need to give himself in agape love moves him as thirst moves a man toward water.

No man who values his ultimate worth and welcomes a release from common anxieties is content with selfish accomplishments. Achievement, as commonly defined, is not engrossing enough. To be known as the richest man in the cemetery would be an unacceptable and repugnant fate. He recognizes as worthless activity the acquisition of life's trinkets or the mere accumulation of academic degrees or other symbols of status.

We need only turn to Solomon to prove his thesis. Flushed with wisdom and laden with gold, he "had it made," yet he was sufficiently discouraged to lament, "Vanity, vanity, all is vanity." Because his motives were selfish, he had spent his life without fulfillment. Until he was restored in relationship to God, misery dogged his life. But even then, his life had been mostly wasted. For he discovered, much too late, that achievement without valid purpose is little more than trash. He ended his life unfulfilled.

Truly unhappy is the person who comes to the end of life with resources unspent. He has missed the opportunity to develop the capacities that were given to him.

Unlike Solomon, the adequate man knows that he must give himself unreservedly to people in agape love. He must achieve that love which is eternally valuable to others and which requires the expenditure of himself. For giving is learned by giving. And usefulness is established by being used. Strong skills and learning factors are involved in selfless giving. Considerable practice is needed to make this mode of life automatic and spontaneous, but with practice the habit of selflessness grows, negating all temptation to return to self-gratification.

Such achievement is spurred by a supreme love of God. It requires the full mobilization of human capacity and creativity, with no resources reserved. This involves loving service, with no thought of reward or reciprocation dominating one's mind. In fact, rewards have a way of detracting from the fulfillment of self-expenditure. Selfless giving can be nullified because others may think that the service was given for reward and not freely.

Instead of visualizing himself as a perpetual giver, the unhappy man perceives himself as a receiver of the symbols of achievement. By constructing a labyrinth of reciprocal agreements, he becomes repository for the Brownie buttons of social recognition: money, status, prestige, achievement. He barters every relationship to produce ego support. In every personal exchange he attempts to secure personal emotional profit. Life is lived as though success consists of a large, identifiable list of credits and assets that the public eye can easily perceive. As a result he has missed the fulfilling joy of total service. Unlike Paul Carlson, his life and his ego are nuclear, not orbital.

What a startlingly different picture we have of Christ. He *emptied* Himself. He allowed Himself to be totally expended in our behalf. It cost Him His life so that we could be the recipients of His supreme love.

In contrast, we spend most of our time trying to *fill* ourselves. Our insatiable appetites seem irreducible. Our consumption of material and psychological goodies appears limitless. We want every emotional kick intensified, and demand endless novelty to keep us satisfied. Soon the supply of life's ticklers is gone, and then we are left with empty cynicism. But what if this insatiable consuming were converted to altruistic, agape-style giving? What would happen?

Obviously our thinking would have to change since the idea of giving ourselves away or of fully expending ourselves is foreign to us. But there is little social pressure on us to be selfless. No current theory of personality or mental health fully accounts for the principle of orbital rather than nuclear personality organization. No body of psychological research has been generated to enlighten us in this area. Hints appear from time to time in humanistic psychology and philosophy, but nowhere is the idea fully developed. Even our humanitarianism, which has obvious appeal because of the great necessity for it, does not satisfy the soul when it is motivated by selfish interests and purely human values. We learn selflessness only through revelation, and it is best explained by the life of Jesus. In selfless giving, He has no peer.

Most textbooks on mental hygiene or human need regard achievement and mastery as ends in themselves. Through achievement man is enhanced and thus satisfied, they conclude. They point to man's continued efforts to produce something or to improve himself as evidence of the need and its validity. But they make no distinction between achievement that is selfish and that which is selfless, a symptom of the life expended in love.

Our thinking, however, must take a different turn. Achievement of ultimate worth is loving self-expenditure, not selfish accumulation. The former is healthy, the latter neurotic. Achievement of living self-expenditure is integrating, wholesome, and redemptive. Achievement for its own sake is selfish, unsatisfying, and ego-inflating. Therefore, two men engaged in exactly the same enterprise, producing the same products or results, can emerge as entirely different psychological and spiritual beings. It all depends on how each man meets his need to be expended.

It is my belief that much of the physical and emotional dissipation we witness derives from a poor and desperate attempt at self-expenditure. It is a neurotic effort, to be sure, but driving needs must be satisfied. We will all be spent, one way or another. Most of us know the problems of someone who has gone down for the final count through alcoholism, mental illness, or even something as socially acceptable as overeating. Failing to expend himself usefully, the person has chosen to dissipate personal resources. The choice is bad, of course, but he had found no other way to be expended.

Some people are so inextricably bound up in themselves that they are unable to consume themselves *except* in dissipation. They have discovered no cause to espouse, no good reason for living. No humanitarian philosophy has satisfied their soul. Hope of fulfillment through agape love and resultant self-expenditure is hidden by ignorance. Nevertheless, their drive to be expended goes unabated. Desperately desiring to be consumed, they make choices that lead to a final resolution.

I believe that this key factor is often overlooked in understanding and treating the alcoholic or addict. While it is well known that the victim may have serious emotional and physiological problems, current theory about healing has not explored the need to be expended. Too many people without serious handicaps, emotional or physical, fall into dissipation. Emotional and physical stress theory is not sufficiently encompassing to explain many of these cases.

In fact, solving some of his emotional problems and achieving physiological stability may deprive such a person of his dissipate methods of expending himself. And this loss hurts terribly. If he has learned to depend on dissipation, he is uncomfortable without it. He is like the neurotic deprived of his irrational behavior. And like the neurotic, he must do *something* to fend off stress. His emotional and physical healing may only sharpen his awareness that life is empty. He is left to face the fact that he knows no reason for his existence. So he returns to dissipation with new vigor, reinforced by a neurotic drive.

In contrast, the New Testament presents a man, the apostle Paul, who is a striking example of one who lived in agape love and productive self-expenditure. He didn't start out that way, however; he changed in adulthood. And this is a most significant psychological fact, for few people reverse the influence of their early lives. Paul's early history must not have been exactly conducive to healthy emotional living. People who turn out as he did have usually been raised by punitive, emotionally cold parents, who also provide a belief system to rationalize their poor child-rearing behavior.

Educated more than most men, Paul was the most feared zealot of his faith. His testimony tells us that he excelled all others in achievement status, religiousness, learning, and pure hostility. The early Christians shuddered at the mention of his name, for he made it his business to jail anyone who opposed him. He consented to the persecution and death of his enemies.

But one day the love of God penetrated his self-righteousness and religious acceptability and turned him around completely. His hostility melted in a new motivation for service. He was so totally permeated with the love of God that he lost no opportunity for self-expenditure. The structure and content of his personality was thoroughly rebuilt. Instead of permitting his life to revolve about his selfish needs and interests, he put his life into orbit around God and loving Him and man.

The degree to which he had been changed is reflected in 2 Corinthians, the fifth chapter. First, Paul carefully explains that who he is and what he is is determined by the love of God and not by human achievements. Then he goes on to tell us what makes him tick. In the thirteenth verse he says, "For if we are beside ourselves (mad as some say), it is for God and concerns Him; if we are in our right mind, it is for your benefit."

Here the apostle Paul implies that he would not struggle or be concerned even to preserve his sanity. His mental equilibrium was God's business, and he was not about to worry himself with the matter. If he was granted the privilege of remaining sound of mind, then it would be totally for the benefit of others. So whether ill or sane, he would give himself away so completely that he would

99

own himself no longer. He reacted as though he had been removed from ownership of self; therefore, he was unconcerned about his personal welfare. He was so completely conscious of his being the object of supreme love, and so totally expended, that he had been released from even the most basic mental concern, the preservation of his mind's equilibrium. His personality had become fully orbital rather than fully nuclear.

Now let's look at another area of expendability.

It is a fact that we become emotionally involved in the things that we own. We attach our feelings of well-being to our possessions. Last winter a mountain cabin we own was threatened by heavy winter snow and rain. We worried about it, wondering if we would lose our investment. Fortunately, no damage was done, and we felt relieved. We had attached feeling to our possession and felt secure when we knew it was safe. But if it hadn't been ours, we wouldn't have worried, for we worry about what we own.

A solution to the worry problem, therefore, is to not be an owner. It is easier not to worry about things we don't own. We can also expend them with much less concern. The same principle applies to our lives. When we are not our own, we need not get excited about our own protection; we can dismiss self-defense. So it was with the apostle Paul. Because he belonged to Christ, he found safety in Him. He also found freedom from self-concern. It became natural for him to give himself away in total expenditure.

If we interpret Paul correctly, we can state a very bold hypothesis. Emotional equilibrium, or peace of mind, or mental health is not an end in itself. Instead it is a by-product of being owned by God and of the loving self-expenditure that so naturally follows. We become so completely free that our very sanity is of little concern. And you won't find a statement like that in any text on personal adjustment!

As a result of our relationship with God, we see our personal stability as a resource to be used in totally consuming altruism. We are blessed with greatly increased ability to give and receive on the basis of agape love. We can take our attention off ourselves and see more of others. Instead of acquiring a tunnel vision, focused constantly on our inner mental gymnastics, we enlarge our horizons to recognize the needs of the world. We see others in need of the same love and freedom from self that we have found. We move toward them, sharing our fulfillment with them, rather than trying to control and rule them and improve their behavior.

You may ask, "What about the person who is on the verge of losing his sanity? Will he not lose it if he surrenders ownership? If he ceases to be concerned for his own stability, will he not slip into psychosis?"

Those of us who have worked with the disturbed and the mentally ill have witnessed their tremendous struggle to keep equilibrium. The sleepless nights, the days filled with tension and fear dominate the mental processes. Raging anger projected on family and friends has strained every relationship. This causes loss of love for the one who needs it most. Few of us are able to supply emotional support for one who is attacking or withdrawing in total fear. Frequently, guilt in the ill person is so great that he indulges in bizarre behavior to alleviate his troubled feelings. How can such a one surrender ownership of self and try to be expendable?

True, there is little available evidence of the therapeutic effects of surrender and expendability in the face of oncoming serious illness. Challenging one to give up sovereignty of self in the face of emotional crisis is not an established therapeutic technique. To make such a challenge requires implicit trust in the direct ability of God to work in a person's life. Further, the method has no evidence in the clinical literature to support it. Instead, the usual approach is to give all possible support to the person in his present understanding. Get him past the crisis and hope that insight can be developed when the situation has calmed.

But I want to share one case with you that suggests the unusual possibilities of expendability as therapy. I was called late one night by a successful executive who wanted help immediately. His wife had been depressed for several weeks and now was in her third day of continuous weeping. Because she hadn't slept nights, every minor incident upset her completely. She couldn't dress the children for school or make out a grocery list. She panicked at the thought of any public appearance, which included stepping outside the house for a minute or two.

This couple experienced added stress because of inability to maintain public appearances. They had stayed away from church for weeks. The husband feared that he might lose his job if the people at work discovered he had an insane wife. And complicating the problem was a compulsion to keep up a good Christian image. After all, when you are a Christian, things like this just don't happen. Isn't it a mockery of your belief and trust? God's strength is supposed to spare or to get one past such troubles.

The husband decided to call me when his wife suggested that either suicide or self-committal to the state hospital was the only answer. Besides, she told him, she was not an adequate wife, and he should have someone as a mate who would be more fulfilling.

When I met with them, we spent several sessions reviewing the personal histories of both the husband and wife, as well as their life as they lived it now. The woman grew up in a large family with a domineering, but withdrawing father. The youngest of eight children, she was lost in the shuffle and suffered a distinct lack of emotional attention. Her mother was the quiet type, always placating the father and keeping the lid on emotional stress in the family.

During college days, the wife had to leave school twice for reasons of fatigue. After a semester of work in business during each period of withdrawal from school, she was able to return and eventually graduated from junior college. In short, her history was indicative of long stress gathered over the years, coupled with low physical stamina. Her tolerance for the current problem was considerably reduced by the same lack of physical stamina.

The difficult birth of their third child precipitated the unceasing tears and sleeplessness. Born prematurely, the child showed no reflex activity that characterizes normal brain function. For three days after the birth she was not shown her baby, nor did she have any word from her doctor. Then suddenly, in a state of high anxiety, he appeared and announced that the child was cerebral palsied. At this point, she nearly lost all self-control.

I spent several interviews with this couple just letting them unburden their accumulated hostility and anxiety. I learned that these people had a genuine knowledge of God and a desire to live for Him. The question became one of how to apply the conceptual knowledge so that it might become a health-giving experience. If this knowledge had not been present, I doubt that we could have taken the adventure that followed.

After some ten hours together, we faced the question of ownership. To whom do we belong? If we are owned by God, then does He not also own our depressed state of mind? Is this not His responsibility? And if He owns us, should we not be willing to accept whatever outcome He has in mind? After considering these questions for some time, I framed the crucial question directly: "Would you be willing to stay in this condition if God, in His sovereignty, so intends? Can ownership of self be so complete that, like the apostle Paul, you will let Him keep you in your right mind if He desires, and if not, let it be His business?"

The crucial question is consistent with the hypothesis we stated earlier: that mental health or peace of mind is a by-product of being owned and expended in agape love. For these folks, this hypothesis had to be acknowledged as critically true or false. If true, they would cease to struggle and take whatever came their way. If false, they would frantically do everything to keep their perceptions intact, making all of life revolve around their critical needs.

Our interviews ceased for about three weeks following the presentation of this important question. Then a call came. "We have decided to try living as Paul suggests," the husband told me. "We believe that God has a direct and personal interest in our welfare."

When this decision was made to put ego into orbit around the will of God, rather than let it occupy a nuclear position, a great sense of peace came. The tears continued to flow for some time, but the fight to resist them was over. The family returned to church even though they could not sit through a service. When they were asked why they always got up and left before any meeting was over, they explained their situation and subsequent decision. Instead of hiding behind masks of tranquility, they began to reveal their true, but difficult lives to friends. The result was an open sharing of problems that brought people together as never before. The fellowship they engendered helped others, who had just as serious problems but who had never had the courage to reveal them.

During the ensuing days, a complete physical checkup was obtained. The family's schedule was modified so that living could be as comfortable as possible. A sister came to live with them and she eased the wife's load considerably. In about three months, recovery was nearly complete.

The decision to expend themselves, both in respect to ownership of self and to service to others, did not magically brush away all the difficulties. Instead it opened a way for healing to occur. It allowed them to reveal themselves and to share both their illness and healing with others. In the years that have followed, this couple has been uniquely equipped to give aid to a number of people who have nearly given up in despair. They now regard those dark days as the greatest blessing God has given to them.

8 Mechanisms and Methods of Adjustment

The human system of obtaining approval involves our use of a number of mental mechanisms. These are spontaneous, often unconscious habits of thought. We are indebted to the discipline of analytic psychology for our understanding of these mechanisms. Knowing that we normally think in ways that incorporate these habits of thought will help us evaluate our own thinking more clearly. Let us list some of them and discuss them one by one.

1. Rationalization: This is the way we make acceptable some deed or event for which we feel guilty or inadequate. I recall vividly the explanations of graduate students who failed to qualify for admission to doctoral studies in the university I attended. We each had to pass a comprehensive examination in the chief areas of our field. It lasted about sixteen hours over a two-day period, and drained our brains of all we knew. It was frightening just to look at the examination room full of people. Every known student with a master's degree and an A-average was there. When the ordeal was over, half of us would be invited to continue. The rest of us would have to rationalize.

"I was just trying out the exams to see how they would go!" offered one unsuccessful venturer. "I plan to give them the full treatment next time they are offered. Now I know what they want from you."

"The University of Colorado seems to have a more realistic approach to these things," suggests another. "I'm already as good as accepted in their program, so this exam doesn't really matter."

"I'm just interested in obtaining the experience," offers another. This last one must have been a masochist. Nobody would endure such agony just for fun.

Rationalization is supplying a seemingly plausible reason for unacceptable behavior. In the face of repeated disappointments, it can become an ingrained process of thought. The habit develops until the person loses his ability to know when he is rationalizing. I have known a few people who rationalize so frequently that their entire mental processes have become distorted. They can seldom think through a problem clearly. Inevitably they choose solutions that seem plausible but that have only a slight chance of being satisfactory. Continually blundering through life, they never understand the reason for their misfortunes.

I once counseled with a police officer who was constantly at odds with his wife. Unable to effect changes in her thinking or behavior, he began to use physical punishment to correct her. He rationalized that her actions were immature. After all, they did not correspond to his authoritative perceptions of the way she should act. Since she was immature, he thought, she should be treated as a child. Therefore, he applied spanking or other punitive measures with increased frequency. Occasionally, she would appear publicly with bruises from her beatings. Needless to say, this marriage ended in a divorce court. Yet the husband could not see any fault of his own. He was merely a concerned mate doing what was obviously best for his wife!

It is obvious to us that serious errors existed in the man's thinking. But he himself didn't see them. His thought system was intact. He had protected his own image as a concerned, caring, thoughtful husband. His rationalization had worked for him. Now he could say that his wife was truly immature and unstable because she was divorcing him. Surely her divorce was a symptom of immaturity!

2. Projection. Blaming others is a simple form of self-defense with which we are all familiar. One summer I coached a Little League baseball team, a venture every father ought to undertake once in his life to learn the full meaning of psychological manipulations of both adults and children. For when we play, we reveal ourselves as we seldom do otherwise.

Our team was blessed with a talented little fellow who in turn was blessed with an overly ambitious mother. She attended every practice, every game, every League meeting, *and* every argument at home plate. In our first critical encounter with cross-town opponents, our budding major leaguer speared a line drive to third base and made an easy double play. All was joy in Mudville for a half-inning! When our turn to bat came, Mr. Athlete, Jr. struck out miserably. He swung at everything including a pitch that landed in the announcer's booth high atop the bleachers. We lost this titanic clash, and mother was livid with rage! Why hadn't proper equipment been provided? Where were the umpires trained? Why were ineligible pitchers allowed to throw to her son? That's right. She was projecting—blaming everyone and everything except the responsible party.

Like rationalization, projecting can become so much a part of thought processes that it is not recognized as such. But a serious secondary aspect of this process should be pointed out. When you project, someone else gets the guff. Someone else's need for protection is needlessly stimulated. No one wants to be crowded into a position of self-defense. Whoever feels the unwarranted blame will return the projections in kind. Have you ever seen much understanding develop in a situation like this? Most fights begin when two people both see themselves as acting in self-defense.

Projection has the distinct disadvantage of creating social stresses needlessly. One may rationalize a good deal as long as no other specific individual is involved. But when we project, others see us as hostile and withdraw from us or retaliate. Our method of protection only complicates the situation. We may save our self-image for the moment, but make enemies doing it.

3. Compensation. The art of building upon our strengths to avoid attention to our weaknesses is called compensation. This can be a useful and helpful way of preserving self-esteem. It can be healthy because growth is frequently involved, and produces legitimate changes in the self-image. We are often better people when we compensate for some flaw. The pages of history frequently describe a great person whose achievements originally began purely as compensation for weakness.

A gentleman I once met was known for his astuteness as a golf coach. His keen eye could detect the subtlest flaw in the swing of one of his students. Professional golfers frequently sought his advice when their games went sour. One day a reporter asked the coach how he had developed such keen abilities. In his reply he related a history of frustration trying to learn the game himself. He simply did not have the physical abilities to execute the complex moves required of a truly great golfer. Instead he compensated. He studied the moves and techniques of all the stars. He trained his eye and his camera to observe the most insignificant detail. The result? Though his own golf game remained good but never excellent, he became a superb teacher.

Compensations, while often useful, can get us into trouble, however. If they contribute to our inability to recognize and correct our weaknesses, we may be better off not compensating. As long as we are reasonably aware of what we cannot do, our compensations will be potentially useful. But when our self-view is badly distorted as the result of compensation, we may have built a trap for ourselves. Our thinking will become habitually unclear, and we may fall victim to the weakness we are trying to overcome.

4. Identification. Recently I read a psychological study about the difference between truly great business executives and those who are mediocre performers or underlings. The study showed that the subordinates and average-quality executives frequently sought satisfaction by identification with more capable men. Rather than achieving purely on their own, they were content to bask in the reflected glory of their superiors and associates. Contrariwise, the outstanding business leaders chose to make their own mark of achievement. While maintaining good relationships with most people, they declined to achieve fame by association.

For example, they avoided certain types of positions. The title "Assistant to the President" carries connotations of reflected glory while the title "Executive Vice-President" carries its own prestige. So the leaders avoided positions with indistinct character and sought out jobs that involved the possibility of unique contribution. Of course, their risk of failure is higher, but their success is not the reflected success of someone else. Success is clearly identified with the person carrying the responsibilities.

As our illustrations indicate, identification is a process of achieving satisfaction through close association with a successful person or organization. While the enjoyment of fulfillment through projection is less than in one's own achievement, the risk of failure is also considerably less. Thus identification meets the needs for protection of the self-image.

When we are identified with a prestigious organization or some famous person, our image improves in our eyes and in the eyes of those who see us. Examples of such

111

identification are everywhere. Students seek an education at Harvard rather than East Overshoe State Technical Institute. Engineers would much rather work for the National Aeronautics and Space Administration than for Ace Doorbell Company. John Q. Adams, IV, will probably attract a different set of girl friends than Joe Schlobowitz. Even the sound of a name attracts or repels people. Most people would rather work for the Peerless Sanitation Engineers than for Bill's Garbage Haulers.

So, our identifications can help us, if they do not block our vision of either our strengths or weaknesses. The reflected glory achieved through stimulating identification spurs us on to meaningful personal achievements. But when our identifications become the chief source of our status and satisfaction, we are in trouble. For then we have traded reality for fantasy and are headed for disaster.

However we may use the mental mechanisms discussed above, or any of the other mechanisms the analytic psychologists suggest, our use of them will probably fall into one of three approaches when we face trouble.

5. Modification. If stress threatens to overwhelm us, we may modify either our perception of the trouble or our perception of ourselves. An example out of today's economic life serves to illustrate.

Newlyweds Cathy and Carl had promised each other the moon. Since both had good jobs, money was no problem, at first. But, as usually happens, Cathy became pregnant, and one income terminated. The fact they had been living on both salaries to make payments on the various parts of the promised moon became chafing sand in their marital bliss. They began sniping at each other and blaming one another for the financial grief. Their strife was at a peak when they glumly sat down before the television set to forget their troubles.

In beautiful living color, a sexy debt merchant showed them how to consolidate all their financial worries in one

112

simple monthly payment and include a new car as a reward for being so intelligent. This seemed to be the answer. Here was a way to modify impending financial doom and postpone the ultimate reality of honeymoon economics. They flew out the door into the clutches of a "financial expert" at the local auto dispensary. The money wizard made good on the TV promise; he sent them home in a new Snortfire Eight with power ash trays and all the other optional equipment. Along with it was a contract for payments somewhat less than they were now expending, *but* with interest, penalties, and a final balloon payoff that would choke a vault at Fort Knox. Cathy and Carl had traded a difficult, immediate problem for an impossible, postponed problem. They had allowed their troubles to modify their perceptions of their difficulties. By modification they temporarily reduced threat and felt more adequate in the present moment. But the ultimate reality was crushing.

Most of us have tried this approach in one way or another. With simple problems it is sometimes useful. We postpone some problems until new, more certain resources are available. But when some major aspect of our lives is at stake, it can be a tragic error. Facing up to tough realities is better than postponing or modifying them into real impossibilities.

6. Denial of self and experience. Once a mother and her eighth-grade daughter sought my counsel concerning a school achievement problem. Apparently the girl had gotten through eight years of elementary education without ever learning to read. Since the initial problem presented to a psychologist is often not the real source of concern, I allowed the conversation to drift into other areas. How was the girl getting along with the other students? What were her ambitions in life?

We had talked rather circuitously for about twenty minutes, when I abruptly asked, "And what does father think about all this?" I should have known better, for any men-

tion of the father in our discussion was conspicuous by
its absence. Immediately mother and daughter burst into
tears as if I were the little Dutch boy who had pulled
his finger out of the dike.

As the discussion continued, I learned that father knew the true nature of the situation, that the child was mentally retarded, but was totally undiplomatic in sharing his knowledge. Instead of being friendly and helpful, he badgered and belittled the child. Though he accepted her retardation, he did so grudgingly.

Mother, suspecting the worst, could not bear the thought that her daughter would never succeed in normal learning requirements. Instead she directed her child to think of becoming a nun where the "only happy life was to be had." A convent would also be a safe place to effect removal of the girl from family embarrassment as well. The approach to the problem was simply to deny that the retardation existed—and to deny father's knowledge of the problem.

Lives that are continually unhappy and disturbed are lives built around a denial of experience. When problems are disclaimed, feelings are swept away and never admitted to conscious experience.

The need to repress many unpleasant emotions leads to insensitivity. Even pleasant feelings can be stifled. People who become insensitive to hurt soon find themselves invulnerable to pleasure as well. The truly free individual hurts a lot because he is willing to admit a full range of feelings to his consciousness. The unruffled stoic often spends great energy denying emotion in order to keep his problems under oppressive control. But while he is doing it, he is temporarily maintaining his image of adequacy and self-control.

A colleague of mine had been a highly successful business executive before entering college teaching. Employed at a high rank and salary, he thought teaching would be a breeze. But his students were bored and bothered with busy work assignments, and nearly revolted one term. The professor, however, refused to recognize the problem. He denied any incompetence on his part and dismissed the students' reactions as frivolous contempt for academic work.

7. Reorganization of perceptions to include the problem. Several years ago we traveled with friends in the mountains, visiting one of our beautiful national parks. Returning from a jaunt to one of the spectacular views at dusk, we marveled at the beauties of the sky. Suddenly a car appeared from the opposite direction, winding crazily up the road. We slowed, pulled to one side, as the auto went by. But then we heard a grinding, scraping sound and the ripping tumult of tires blowing out. The approaching car had struck the vehicle just behind us. Fortunately no injuries occurred, but the collision accomplished some inartistic engraving on both autos.

Both drivers emerged, the man from the offending car indisputably under the influence of liquor. They exchanged information about drivers' licenses and insurance policies. Others helped make arrangements to remove the damaged vehicles and transport the passengers to their destinations.

The event had fairly well spoiled our recollections of a beautiful day as we sat around camp that evening expressing thankfulness that no one had been hurt. We assumed the event was a matter of the past and decided to forget it.

Not so. Two weeks after we had returned home, our doorbell rang, and there stood a constable. He handed me papers that said I was being sued by someone for "permanent bodily damage and grievous physical pain and suffering" to the tune of $15,000. Suing me! I wasn't in any accident! Why me?

My first impulse was to ignore the whole silly business. Obviously it was a mistake and would take care of itself. Furthermore, it was the drunk who was doing the suing, and obviously he couldn't collect! In short, my impulse was either to modify my perceptions into some safe kind of experience or to deny the existence of a problem alto-

116

gether. I was not going to give this trauma the courtesy of being thought of as some honest reality.

I mentioned the matter to my golf partner a day or so later and, to my surprise, he said, "You had better see a good lawyer, buddy." Me, see a lawyer? I didn't believe in paying people to defend me against nothing! My golf partner was adamant. Since I had to do something, I decided to turn the matter over to my insurance carrier, even though the whole business was completely unfair.

When I called my agent that evening, he assured me I had done the right thing and that suits of this kind came up rather frequently. I still struggled to believe it. But it is a good thing I did, for the insurance company spent a substantial number of hours straightening out the whole mess. It seems that the drunken driver who was trying to sue me had mistakenly mixed up the license numbers of the cars. The car he had struck was the same make as mine. Since he also had my name as a witness it was easy for him to get thoroughly confused and direct the litigation at the wrong man.

But suppose I had persisted in my plans just to ignore the whole mess? I might have been involved in endless details and nuisances. It took some stimulating, but I had to accept the fact that I was the subject of litigation and needed to respond appropriately. I had to reorganize my thinking to include the very real fact that a problem was immediately before me and had to be faced. My denial of responsibility did not change the fact I was being sued.

Many people's perceptions are so rigid that they automatically refuse to recognize serious problems. In fact, some persons no longer understand that they are unaware. They have experienced so much stress in the past that their minds block out the truth, making no attempts at reorganization.

The psychologically able individual usually reorganizes his thinking to account fully for the problems thrust upon him. He deals with them rationally, sensing all the related emotions. Then he resumes his normal experience. He is not so insulated from the stress he feels that he spontaneously ignores reality, or modified through safe but unrealistic perceptions.

Another problem occurs in all our lives when we have to choose between perceived alternatives. As we develop from small children into adulthood, we become strongly involved in the lives of our family members. These strong ties frequently involve a considerable mixture of emotions. We are dependent on them and loving toward them, yet often at odds with them and seeking independence from them. In short, the elements of love and hate, hurt and joy, exist side by side in these intense relationships. These competing emotions are probably strongest during adolescence, when emotional divorce from parents and family is a natural and desirable occurrence.

When a loved one dies, however, we struggle with a certainty that challenges us in our perceptual capacities. Only the most confused person can fully deny such reality in his experience. Yet, accepting the full reality is also a difficult step to take. In some way or other, most of us deal with the problem by modifying it into a more acceptable experience. If the loved one has been ill, we may pretend to be glad that he is gone, telling ourselves that he is better off where he is now. Or, as some stoics say, "Everyone's number comes up sometime." In any event, most people modify perceptions first, then ease themselves into the full reality of the experience. I think that this is why some people experience considerable grief long after the event has taken place. They have modified their perceptions by postponing their reactions. Or they have continued certain rituals of their lives, retaining some part of previous experience that involved the one deceased.

Eventually, the full reorganization must come, or life proceeds with distortion and discomfort. Most of us know of someone who, having lost a loved one, closeted himself in his home within his feelings and failed to respond to much of anything forever after.

The denial or modification of our perceptions of experience hampers us in the fortunate experiences of life as well. Earlier, we pointed out that the truly free person hurts a lot because his openness makes him aware of a wide range of human experience. People who have been continually threatened emotionally become so protective that they lose their capacities to revel in joy as well as suffer pain. For them, happiness involves the risk of relationship, and this may be too distressing. Too many unfortunate contacts with people in the past have built emotional callouses to feelings of all kinds.

The mental gymnastics we go through in seeking adequacy become, in themselves, evidence of the extreme nature of our need for adequacy. Ernest Hemingway is reported to have said, in effect, that destruction is more acceptable than defeat. From our observations of the seriously troubled, we conclude that they often choose insanity instead of reality, if reality reveals them to be inadequate. Self is so clearly at the center of existence that the world must be blocked out before it can admit inadequacy. Or self must be distorted into acceptability so the world cannot touch it no matter what its character may be.

9 The Nature of the Redemptive Relationship

Listening is the key to the redemptive relationship. Listening is the means by which we gain entry to each other's lives. But what we do on admittance is also critically important. It is possible to play the role of listener and then become destructive when the one to whom we are listening becomes vulnerable to us. Listening must be accompanied by other behaviors to insure that the relationship remains helpful.

A young college girl returned home for Christmas after one quarter in a Midwestern university. It had been a difficult term for her; she had experienced both academic and social difficulties. Her grades were below par, and she had been placed on academic probation. Coming from a protective environment, totally surrounded by church people, she had little knowledge of the worldly sophistication of urbane, mod groups that populate our cities. Lonely and uninitiated, she had fallen for a number of temptations that went against her moral convictions. She had tried to relate to others, but her new friends had only exploited her naiveté.

121

LISTENING

She made an appointment with her minister one morning shortly after returning home. She struggled with herself wondering how to get out the words of confession and how to plead for help. When she arrived at the church office at the appointed hour, the pastor invited her in. "How's our pride and joy?" he inquired warmly. "It will be good to hear how you've gotten along."

"I'm a mess," she blurted. "Between liquor and sex, I can hardly stand myself!"

"What? You, the most stable and mature Christian girl in our church! You should be ashamed of yourself," he retorted. She leaped from her chair and ran out the door, tears streaming from her eyes.

The minister lost his opportunity to be redemptive the moment he became judgmental. His spontaneous outburst of rejection of the girl gave himself away. He was a moralist and a legalist who accepted only those people who conformed to his codes. Pharisaical in attitude, he thought he was doing God a favor with his pronouncements.

It is questionable whether he or those in his church had ever been redemptive in the life of the girl. This congregation respected people only if they turned out "right" according to predetermined stereotypes. All others were spiritual inferiors whose faith was suspect.

The girl left the church entirely and turned to a group of self-styled intellectuals for her answers. In their presence, her sin was acceptable and her problems were dealt with in cool philosophical fashion. Ignoring the need for real resolution of guilt, she became a suave sophisticate who was above such silly things as archaic moralisms.

The redemptive relationship is a nonmoralizing relationship. People who seek help from others are often driven by guilt. In remorse they yearn for help. When the first reaction is judgment of guilt or moral disapproval, they feel rejected. Their grief is intensified so greatly that their only recourse is withdrawal. Opportunity for redemption is lost.

In chapter 3, we discussed how you can avoid love by becoming moral. Being moral will make you moralistic if love and guilt resolution are not part of the morality. In your self-styled purity you will either require the same attitude from others or you will reject them. Those who disagree with you will become reminders of your own sin. It is a psychological fact that judgmental, moralistic people are often those with the most unresolved guilt to hide. And people who hide can scarcely be redemptive.

A judgmental attitude toward others puts them on the defensive. They feel insulted or hurt. In this emotional posture, they cannot be open to emotional healing. They are too busy protecting themselves, too occupied with maintaining self-esteem. Defensiveness of personality, therefore, is the antithesis of growth, for growth only occurs when defenses are lowered.

The redemptive relationship is not a coercive relationship. One does not feel overwhelming pressure to be what he cannot be. Instead he has the sensation of being gently led. He is drawn by another who has ventured into growth and who knows the way. He is drawn to move as quickly as he can feel comfortable and as quickly as he can comprehend his own emotions about growing.

In contrast, the coercive person insists that all problems must be solved immediately and on his terms. No latitude for error is allowed. No freedom to approach and withdraw from potential solutions. Just follow the right formula and get on with it. Further, progress must proceed along lines he has already defined with his own jargon. A limited set of terms and concepts must be used. If others are attempted, the coercive person regards it as a form of heresy. Whether any set of terms really defines growth or not is debatable. Sometimes people assume that they have grown simply because they can use the new colloquialisms in their vocabulary.

We run across examples of this problem in counseling psychology. Occasionally I will see a person who uses the jargon of psychology so well that I am tempted to believe they have insight into their problems. They speak in detail of their Oedipus complex, overlays of reaction formation behavior, and resultant neurotic stress. But when it comes to doing something about their condition, they blame their parents and environment, and then seek someone else with whom to have a catharsis. Maybe someone else will equate their use of psychological jargon with growth.

In the New Testament we see Jesus bumping into a similar problem. He had most of His problems with the religious conservatives of His day who knew all the words, but whose lives were a bit of death warmed over. The same is true today. I suspect those who parade religious and theological jargon, but who seldom make any emotional progress in their lives—the hateful heresy-hunters and doctrine-dictators who get along with no one.

Pressure to manifest quickly stereotyped symptoms of progress, along with the use of some particular jargon, usually comes from someone who is more coercive than redemptive. This need to be coercive is itself a symptom of insecurity, an insecurity that the person compensates for by attempting to be dominant or sovereign in the emotional experiences of others.

The redemptive relationship is an equalitarian relationship. While no two people in the world have the same fingerprints, aptitudes, physical characteristics, or social opportunities, a more important quality than any of these is the privilege of all of us. We are equally the objects of the love of God. We are equally entitled to grow in our knowledge of Him and in our personal lives. We are equally entitled to see ourselves as the objects of His grace, and not as advantaged or disadvantaged by some human standard.

When the relationships among a group of people or with another individual become dominated by this sense of equality, a redemptive spirit results that affirms the person. Whatever our backgrounds, we are entitled to affirmation by God and man. To be redemptive is to respond primarily to the equalities of people and their common need for love. While much work is needed in the area of human rights and social justice, it is possible to become so preoccupied with the inequalities of man that we miss the basis for our most redemptive activity, the true equality that exists among men.

Recently we acquired a very standard model of gray kitten in our home. He was only a few weeks old when he arrived, but he quickly caught the attention and affection of our children. They noticed that he had a particular way of becoming acquainted with strangers and with the new items in his environment. He would quietly sneak up on one of them, and then quickly withdraw when a response was made. As he grew in courage, he would come closer and remain longer. Eventually, he became so sure of himself that only a serious jolt could get him off one's lap or away from something breakable.

People behave in much the same way. They approach and withdraw from the objects and persons they are attempting to get to know. In overcoming fears of specific things or experiences, the freedom to approach and withdraw is most helpful. Thus, it is also a characteristic of the redemptive relationship. If we would truly be helpful, we must grant people the opportunity to approach and withdraw from both the problem and the solution required.

Most people have mixed feelings about solving a problem. When problems are solved, relationships change. And this change upsets our stability of perception. An old saying has it that we fear less the devils we know than the angels we don't know. To solve a problem is to risk new terms of relationships. It also usually means deeper and more meaningful relationships with more possibility to both help and hurt. This can create a definite feeling of anxiety. As a result, some people actually resist solving problems while apparently trying to solve them. It's the old story of mixed emotions—as when your wealthy mother-in-law names you as heir and then comes to live with you.

When people do not respect the needs others have to approach and withdraw from a problem, it usually means that the supposed helper or helping group is becoming coercive. They would rather see someone progress and be able to call themselves successful than to allow the troubled individual to work through his situation at his own pace.

But when we become redemptive, we allow others to have as much "wiggle room" as they need. We do not insist on symptoms of progress to prove our own worth as helpers. In fact we must be willing to let the person fail, if he insists. If we do not, we are usurping the rights of sovereignty over the person's life. And only God is entitled to that. Further, only the person himself can give back to God his personal sovereignty.

A redemptive relationship is a series of shared experiences. As such, it is not always smooth and velvety. Sharing some things precludes easygoing occasionally. When life is fully shared, things get abrasive from time to time. If they don't, there is some evidence of withholding oneself in the relationship. And this leads us to a problem.

I was speaking on the subject of marriage and home matters in a church one Sunday evening. Prior to my address, the group had gathered for coffee and cake. We chatted awhile, getting acquainted with the people and enjoying good fellowship. During the conversation, one particularly affluent gentleman announced that his only problems were financial, and that most of those could be laid at the feet of organized labor. He was happy that I was there to speak about marriage, but he assured me that most of what I said probably wouldn't apply to him.

Announcements like this always make me wonder a bit, perhaps even stimulate me to do a better-than-average job with the subject. At any rate, we did have a very good session. I felt happy about my presentation, and the audience entered into a question-and-answer period with considerable enthusiasm. Especially involved was the man who had announced that his only problems were financial. From time to time he would make a statement or ask a question that revealed a bit of his hidden self. Then after the meeting he cornered me and we began an hour's discussion.

"My wife is very nervous," he indicated. "She always seems upset, especially at bill paying time and tax time. I tell her not to worry, everything will go all right, and we'll have plenty to live on. We always do, too, you know."

"You share your financial worries with her, then?" I questioned.

"Yes, but I don't really bother her with them. I just let her in on enough to keep her interested in my work."

"What else do you share with her in your life?" I continued. Counselors find that the problem presented to them is often a test case to see if the real problem will be carefully handled. Perhaps financial problems were only an opening scene to the real drama in this life.

The gentleman was visibly shaken by my question, though it seemed innocent enough to me. Instead of pursuing an answer, he talked disinterestedly again about money matters. Then he thanked me for my presentation and dismissed himself.

I learned later that his wife had sought the counsel of

her minister because of feelings of great loneliness. She was completely left out of her husband's life. When he mentioned financial problems to her, it made her anxious, not because money worried her, but because it was the only part of his life she really knew about. When the subject came up, she was hopeful that it might be a beginning of extended discussion in other personal areas. In her hopefulness she was showing her anxiety. The response of her husband to the anxiety was not to open up more, but to limit even the discussions of money. As a result they shut each other out of their inner lives, and the wife found herself a lonely woman with no one to share life with her.

I learned later, too, that the husband had had a serious problem getting along with his employees. He either ingratiated himself with them or provoked them sorely. Then I began to wonder how his life and his marriage might have been different if this abrasive problem had been shared with his wife rather than hidden. It might have been tough to discuss a personal weakness and arguments might have ensued. But had the effort been made, the wife would have not experienced loneliness and her husband might have found real help in their relationships. The opportunity for redemptive relationship in marriage had been missed because only the pleasantries had been exchanged and none of the abrasiveness was allowed admittance.

When we act redemptively toward others, in marriage, in personal encounter, or in fellowship and sharing groups, we come out best by sharing the full spectrum of our lives. This requires a good deal of risk, for in admitting others to areas of our personal vulnerability we can get hurt. But if the final outcome is to be growth, the risk must be taken.

For the sake of easy moments, and perhaps for the appearance of social acceptability, we often become limited-spectrum people. Only those areas of life that are already comfortable to us are open for examination and relationship. The full spectrum of our experiences is kept available. To escape this truncated growth, there are at least two steps we must take.

First, recall that the words of Jesus were, "I am come that you might have life and have it more abundantly." (See John 10:10.) It is a solemn promise of God to give you life if you will have it. But you must make the move to open yourself to Him. And He is no threat. He accepts us for what we are without retribution and makes it safe for us to go into His presence without anxiety. Then as we become sure of ourselves with Him, we can begin to work through our problems on a no-risk basis, knowing that He will act redemptively toward us.

The second step follows the first. When we have been assured by God of our acceptability to Him, it is easier to share our lives with other people, especially with those who have decided to pursue a course similar to the one we have taken. God uses other people to help us. And in sharing redemptively with them, we help them, too.

The redemptive relationship is one in which no one calls the shots. No one prescribes behaviorally defined objectives that all must pursue. The prevailing attitude is that each person is a unique creation, to be perfected in God's own way and manner, and that anything short of this is a truncated growth experience. Each grants the other maximum freedom to be uniquely individual in the hands of the Master Creator.

Too often more limited results occur. It is easy for us to become so preoccupied with the behavioral definitions of our belief systems that we look only for certain behaviors as symptoms of growth. Further, we insist that growth and feeling must be expressed in rigid concepts, using a standardized vocabulary. A kind of personal theology appears more trustworthy than the Person of God. Systems then take priority over people, even in religious and psychological experience. It ought not to be so.

When we impose limited objectives and specifically defined behavioral requirements upon people, we lapse into the tendency to become coercive. We subtly insist that we would like to have a bit of control over others. Somehow we cannot trust ourselves to other people until we have at least a limited sovereignty over their lives. Again, this is the antithesis of growth. Sovereignty of persons belongs to God alone, or to the person himself, if he is so shortsighted as to not give it up to the Creator.

Finally, the redemptive relationship is one that can be terminated without guilt. This condition of relationship is consistent with our understanding of agape love. This love is freely given and freely received. It is reciprocal love that solicits obligation. Reciprocal love is a necessary love in the conduct of human affairs, but for fully redemptive purposes, a higher order of relationship must exist.

Some relationships must be discontinued simply because we move about, change human status, play new roles. Sometimes growth depends on terminating a relationship that has outgrown its redemptive and helpful characteristics. If relationships continue only to fulfill mutual obligation, they quickly lose any capacity for redemptiveness they might have had. Thus they are best terminated.

We have friends who live in Asia that we rarely see. Further, we correspond once every two years, if at all. But when they come home, we immediately seek each other out and have the time of our lives. We can pick up the conversation where we left it five years before when they were last home. We help them some, financially, but otherwise we make little contact while they are away. Their friendship has been one of the greatest sources of help and blessing to our lives. But one important factor is apparent. We are free to take leave of each other and to resume fellowship with each other on the freest of terms.

130

We begin and end in a redemptive way, and our lives are far richer for the experience.

Perhaps the best description of conditions for redemptive relationships is found in 1 Corinthians 13:1, "If I speak in the tongues of men and of angels. . . ."

10 *The Need for Physical Well-Being and Security*

I was beginning my first responsibility as a school psychologist when one of our principals called me for quick assistance. He did not explain his problem fully, so I hurried to his school as rapidly as possible. Arriving just as classes were beginning, I found one teacher and her class locked out of their room. The principal and teacher were struggling with the lock, which some unknown culprit had obviously jammed from the inside. The janitor came by shortly and was able to get us into the classroom. The first of the children filed in, then burst back into the corridor shrieking. Flying music books barely skimmed their heads as they attempted to enter.

Shielding myself, I volunteered to recapture command of the halls of academia. Once inside I found a husky boy, music books in hand, standing on top of the upright piano ready to let fly. When he saw me, he quickly ducked away, hiding behind the piano and window draperies close by. I approached him carefully, seeking an explanation for the small riot he had created. He cowered in the corner, muttering that he knew I was after him and must be intent on punishing him. He was partly correct, but I assured him

133

that I wanted to hear what he had to say before I took any action.

The principal ushered him to the office and we spent several minutes calming him down. Then I questioned the teacher about her experiences with the child previously. "Is this the first such outburst you have experienced?" I asked.

"No, not really, I had him in kindergarten a couple of years ago and he was a terror then," she replied. "His school record is written in teachers' sweat."

The boy, whom we'll call Richard, was the best-known student in this elementary school. Every teacher who had taught him, or had been on yard duty, knew of his antics. He was usually referred to as the worst behavior problem in the school and with a near perfect attendance record! His fame spread to the neighborhood as well. He had the reputation of a sulking bully who believed everyone was picking on him.

A day later, I called at the home to see how the parents had been able to work with him. Mother proved to be a weary and frustrated woman, not knowing where to turn for help. She wasn't sure she wanted to see anyone from school because such visits just meant more trouble. As is customary in case work, I also asked some details about the boy's health history and emotional development. Giving the mother the details about the recent incident at school I asked, "What is Richard's usual reaction to difficult situations?" With this she sensed that I was not there to level judgment, but to learn all I could about her boy.

The story was a long one, but the salient points were very meaningful and formed a diagnostic constellation frequently found in high-strung children like Richard. While living in another state, the boy had been seriously ill with a kidney infection. The resultant high fever and delirious condition warranted immediate hospitalization. The boy lapsed into a coma for several days, and doctors wondered whether he would recover. But the crisis passed and Richard returned home, apparently recovered. Shortly after hospitalization, he experienced several severe convulsive episodes. Later neurological examinations confirmed that some brain damage had probably resulted from his serious illness.

The mother also indicated that Richard's personality underwent considerable change after the hospitalization. He had been a placid child until that time, but now many things upset him. His emotions seemed to be on a Yo-Yo, and his moods were unpredictable. He seemed possessed by a hair-trigger temper that flared at the most inopportune times. In school he had the most difficulty learning to translate his thoughts into writing as they came to him. Writing a simple paragraph, dictated by the teacher, was an impossible assignment. But his mathematical abilities seemed to have remained intact. Summer vacations took an unusual toll in loss of learning. It seemed as though he had to learn to read all over again every fall.

But the most difficult factor to deal with was the explosive personality. Class members could never predict his reactions, and because he was strong and husky, they learned to fear him. As a result, they withdrew, and Richard found himself with very few friends. This fact became important in his outlook on life, for he began to feel inferior and easily hurt. In retaliation for his injured feelings, he would abuse classmates, often hurting them painfully.

Richard and his family were advised to seek the services of a diagnostic center at a large hospital, where both psychological and physical factors could be evaluated. This study would give us full information on how to help Richard make the most of school as well as of his personal life. As we suspected, significant brain damage was noted, along with the usual corresponding symptoms: moodiness, temper, impaired general coordination, flight of attention, to mention a few. With a carefully controlled medication program consisting mainly of anticonvulsants and mild depressants, behavior was brought under control, and the boy's attitude improved markedly. He no longer flared at slight provocations. Children lost much of their fear of him, and his social life returned to near normal. No longer a sulking bully, he felt as though he had achieved a major personal victory in life.

It would have been easy to label Richard an obstreperous boy and prescribe only punishment. I often wonder how many other needy boys have never had the benefit of full understanding and modern facilities, and so have lived out their lives in unhappiness. It became clear that Richard's problem was basically a physical problem, not a psychological one. His behavior was merely a symptom of an underlying physical condition.

As I worked with the family for several years, I was impressed with their stability and genuine concern. The parents were not the kind one would expect to have a boy with difficult behavior. But behavior, all behavior is built upon a physiological basis and this basis must not be overlooked. In Richard's case it provided the key to a most happy solution, not only for Richard, but for the parents who were feeling guilt and failure that was unjustified.

No behavior, including thought and emotion, occurs apart from tissue. Mind and body are one in structure, and highly related in function. When one goes out of kilter, the other is affected. No psychological diagnosis is complete without full recognition of the physiological factors underlying behavior. And no one can be a fully developed person without proper physical well-being. Man clearly needs physical security and stability.

Few machines run in such a delicate balance as does the human body. The smallest change in functioning is often felt immediately. As I sit typing this chapter, I am mindful of the fact that I forgot my thyroid pill this morning. I'm a little slow of mind and keep pressing the wrong keys. Something is out of balance and I'll need to correct matters shortly. But the best example is how we feel when our body temperature varies about two degrees. How do you feel then? If you are normal, a two-degree elevation will put you in bed for at least twenty-four hours.

Yet I see many people who take very poor care of themselves and wonder why they are upset, depressed, or just miserable. This is especially true of college students who delight in burning the candle at both ends. One young psychology major stopped by my office to complain that he was losing interest in school. He liked his major and wasn't thinking of changing, but he just seemed to lack motivation. "Give me an idea of your schedule," I said.

"Oh, I am taking nineteen units this quarter and working part time," he replied.

"How long and when?" I asked.

"I finish classes about four-thirty, and I work at a laundry from six in the evening until one in the morning. I sleep until seven and get to school at eight."

"How much sleep do you actually get?" I questioned further.

"Well, I'm engaged, and have to see my girl some time, so I usually stop by her house after work for about an hour."

"Then you sleep?"

"Yes, about four hours a night, if I'm lucky!"

"And you are wondering why you are not motivated? Can I make a guess?" My question obviously rubbed him the wrong way.

As it turned out, he was unhappy about being engaged, and he was using the work excuse to keep from seeing his girl any more than he had to. He seemed to lack the courage to break off the relationship. He just hoped she would get tired of his visits at one o'clock in the morning and perform the break-off surgery herself. In time, however, they managed to separate, and the boy's motivation increased markedly, as well as his sleeping time. He got another job, happily resumed his studies and obtained outstanding grades.

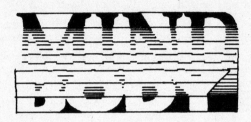

A psychiatrist friend of mine who works in a large university reports that he frequently sees students who eat poorly, sleep little, indulge in undisciplined fun, and then wonder why they are depressed. "The fact is," he says, "you just can't get kids to realize that feelings are based on physical functioning. If you tax your physical capacities, you are going to feel bad."

One quiet evening the phone rang as we were about to retire. A friend I had known for a long time was calling, and it was obvious that he was in a state of controlled desperation. "Ever have your wife talk of committing herself?" he asked, trying to insert a little humor into his desperation. "I know some guys who would relish the idea, but I don't! What do I do, Doc?"

"Tell me what's going on," I replied.

"Well, she feels so low she won't risk leaving the house. She cries all the time and doesn't want me to go to work. Then she says she can't pray, feels nobody could love her, and wants me to put her away. I've never been through anything like this. It just doesn't seem real. I hear about others having such troubles, but I never thought it would happen to us."

I asked a number of questions to sort out possible emotional factors from physical factors before making a suggestion. Since the surface indications were that no great psychological trauma was present, I urged them to seek out a specialist in internal medicine. Sure enough, he found the answer. The woman was seriously lacking in thyroid production. After several sessions of lab work, the doctor prescribed medication, principally thyroid. In a matter of weeks, the depression had gone, and the family was back on an even keel.

Obviously, not every case responds to treatment so dramatically as this one. But whenever there is some significant shift in emotional well-being, you should have a thorough checkup by a medical doctor. Take a look at the following list of symptoms. These describe a significant number of people who request appointments with me.

—Appointment usually sought by a woman. Men scarcely ever call psychologists. They come after their wives get involved.
—Feelings of depression and worthlessness.
—Seriously overweight or underweight.
—Inability to sleep.
—History of uncertainty as a child resulting from emotionally unresponsive parents.
—Many financial and social obligations that seem never to end.
—Several children born within a short period of years; little time between pregnancies.
—Some major surgery accompanying onset of symptoms. Often a hysterectomy, or other procedure involving glands.
—An unsupportive mate who retreats in time of stress.

Just reading the list makes me tired. No wonder people with such a parade of symptoms hurt emotionally. They are pooped, exhausted, joyless. Even faith seems to have vanished, and they have run out of theological answers to life.

I was discussing this list with physicians at a nearby mental health center as we were reviewing the kind of patient who seeks help. One of the doctors piped up, "Sounds like fifty percent of my practice!"

"Mine, too," said another.

Obviously, you shouldn't do any self diagnosing from this list, but anytime a significant emotional change occurs in just a few weeks, a thorough checkup is highly recommended. I have seen too many people change theology, assume highly modified self-concepts, break up marriages, or fight with their in-laws as a result of a physical disorder. It is amazing to see the reaction when the problem is corrected. I recall one particularly distraught woman, who divorced her husband and abandoned her children only to find that she had been given some very bad advice and that essentially she had a physical problem, not an emotional one. It took months, but eventually the hurts were healed sufficiently for the couple to remarry and resume a normal home life.

Following is another list. These are cases I have known in the past with their chief symptoms and causes. All were more complex than I am indicating, but I am oversimplifying to make a point.

—A kindergarten girl with a subnormal IQ. After three years of specific endocrine treatment, her intelligence returned to normal.
—A leader in a women's organization was known for her extreme Christian enthusiasm and high rate of activity. Nobody could keep up with her. A glandular condition propelled her until she was exhausted and had to be hospitalized.
—A junior-high-school boy developed a serious inferiority complex. He piled on fat about the waist, but not on his extremities. Embarrassed about his appearance, he

became painfully shy. Studies revealed a serious hypo-thalamic condition.

—An elderly woman seriously considered suicide as a result of episodes of depression. Hating all doctors except veterinarians, she refused medical attention. Eventually she lapsed into a coma and was rushed to a hospital where severe diabetes was diagnosed.

—A fourth-grade boy frequently appeared to experience mild seizures. Referred to a diagnostic center, he was found to suffer from extremely serious vitamin deficiencies.

—A third-grade boy couldn't read, and failed every subject. He fell over objects and ran into things. He was referred to the psychologist as possibly retarded. When fitted with a pair of glasses with a built-in hearing aid, his IQ and achievement returned to normal.

When the need for physical stability is not met, a number of psychological factors come into play. These factors are attempts at solving the problem, but will always prove unsatisfactory until the root problem is solved. Occasionally we are able to detect subtle physiological difficulties by closely observing the psychological processes of the mind. Under persistent physical stress, any one or several of the following psychological symptoms may occur.

1. Reduced mobility. We easily identify this symptom in the aged. No one really wonders why an elderly person does not leave the house very much. It exposes him to illness and danger. But when a younger person spends too much time at home, we have cause to wonder. Reduced mobility shuts off the individual from people. Thus he lacks the reassurance of friends. He fails to achieve the proper rewards for his efforts. His personal life becomes impoverished, and he is lonely. In his withdrawal, he becomes unhappy and wonders why the world is such an unfriendly place. In time, his whole personality suffers distortion.

2. Restricted interests. When physical problems plague

a person, too much of his attention must be given to his own body and mind. Busily introspecting about how he feels, he becomes preoccupied with pain and discomfort. Self-concern soon permeates his personality, and he focuses almost entirely on his selfish interests. As a result, he loses touch with current happenings in his social world and is less conversant about happier matters. Others find him uncomfortable to be around and withdraw, leaving him to his loneliness. One oldster in a retirement home complained, "All I hear about around here are problems of the lower intestinal tract and the way the Democrats are ruining the country."

The person who has successfully overcome a physical handicap knows that he must constantly work at not thinking of himself in terms of his handicap. It is quite a different matter to think of oneself as a handicapped person rather than as a person with a handicap. A person with a handicap does not lose his ability to think straight, or his ability to make acquaintances, or his capacity to establish fulfilling activities in his experience.

3. Truncated judgment. This is a subtle process, but it exists nevertheless. By *truncated,* we mean restricted, accounting for less than the whole of the matter. A physically beset individual tends to make decisions about himself in terms of his limits rather than his possibilities. In so doing, he probably restricts his life and limits himself needlessly.

Examples of distorted judgment related to deprivations are documented in psychological research. We know for example that very poor children perceive coins to be larger than they really are. We know that starving people dream of steaks and caviar rather than hamburger and beans. Impoverished people see moderately built homes as fine estates. All of our judgments reflect our problems, and our problems can so preoccupy us that we make bad decisions.

Changes in ability to make judgments occur slowly and

142

often without the awareness of the person. Efforts are necessary to guard against this possibility. Anyone constantly bothered by a serious problem would do well to seek professional counsel just to check his judgment ability.

4. Resistance to correction. To make a satisfactory correction in thinking requires the admission of possible error in judgment. This can be guilt-provoking and therefore may be resisted, especially if the judgment was particularly bad. For some, the cure is more painful than the kill. Further, to correct an underlying physical problem is to risk finding out how serious things may be. Thus the problem may be doubly resisted.

I recall the case of a woman who was feeling very low and began to blame her husband's employment for her stress. If only he would change work so they could live somewhere else. So they moved, but no relief came. She nagged for a second move, then a third, and still no relief. In time, medication and rest effected a satisfactory solution. Now she was very chagrined because of the insults and nagging she had leveled at her husband for not appreciating how she felt and suggesting that the problem was within

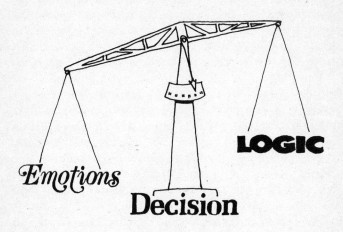

her and not him. We both assured her that we were happy she was well and that she should forget her embarrassment. But it wasn't enough. Now we get a box of candy every Christmas to atone for the misbehavior during counseling sessions.

The fact remains that we believe in the way we feel. Our feelings take precedence over logic in personal decision-making. And when we are ill, we make decisions that correspond with that illness and not always with the inherent logic of the matter. It takes considerable self-objectivity to seek correction in thinking and feeling, even when obvious physical ills may explain the condition.

11 Biblical Grounds for Self-Identity

In chapter 4 we pointed out that all of us need to see ourselves as adequate people. Without perceived self-adequacy, we are largely doomed to failure. The inadequate self-picture becomes the self-fulfilling prophecy of disappointment. On the other hand, a self-image of adequacy gives rise to feelings of success and optimism. Again a self-fulfilling prophecy is at work. One who predicts success for himself tackles tough projects, attempts difficult tasks, and often obtains elusive and valuable goals that most others miss.

A good self-image does not mean lifting oneself by one's bootstraps. A good self-image develops out of valid information about oneself. If a person has a good self-image, he has fully accepted the truth about himself, and that truth is not demeaning. Neither is it a delusion of success where none exists. A good self-image must be based on a genuine and honest self-appraisal. Otherwise the resulting disappointments will be doubly damaging, and ultimate recovery will be most difficult.

Self-appraisal is the way you value yourself. It's the way you see yourself, both implicitly and explicitly. It's the kind of terms you choose to describe yourself. It's the picture of yourself you carry in your mind. But the question is, is it a true picture or a false one? By what standard do you judge yourself—by man-made goals and values, or by enduring, eternal truth? What is the hard ground of reality about you? What is the most believable thing that can be said about you?

My attention was first drawn to this question when I was a freshman in college. It was Christian Emphasis Week on campus, and a guest speaker in chapel had posed the question, "Who do you think you are, anyway?" It is not unusual for a college freshman to tackle this question. In fact, life away from home with new friends and peers and new intellectual expectancies is bound to raise questions about self-identity. The first year of college provides both an unusual opportunity for self-discovery and a risky trial for the more uncertain student.

The basic tenet of Professor Arthur Combs' book, *Individual Behavior,* is that we behave in terms of the way we see ourselves. If we want to predict anyone's behavior, we must know how he sees himself in the situation where the behavior is going to take place. No other single bit of information about a person is so vital and useful for prediction purposes. Knowledge about IQ, grades, socioeconomic status, and the like is helpful, but not nearly so useful as the knowledge of self-image. Our Christian Emphasis speaker put it this way:

The philosopher says, "I am what I become. . . ."
The capitalist says, "I am what I own. . . ."
The scholar says, "I am what I know. . . ."
The existentialist says, "I am what I perceive and feel. . . ."
The moralist says, "I am what I do. . . ."
The radical says, "I am not what I reject!"

But Paul, the apostle says, "I am the least of the apostles, unfit to be called an apostle, because I persecuted the church of God. But by the grace of God I am what I am" (1 Cor. 15:9-10).

The point of the text is that Paul had learned to see himself primarily as an object of God's grace. No longer

I GOD

GOD RIGHTEOUS

did he view himself as a Jew, a Pharisee, an intellectual, or a persecutor, for now he was an object of the supreme love of God. All other evidence to the contrary, his first business was to assume that he was as like Christ as possible, because that is the way God regarded him.

The fact that Paul could identify himself as the object of the grace of God in no way denies other possible facets of self-image. He was not covering up anything, he was simply acquiring a more important, more dominant factor in his self-description than he had known before. As a result he could spare himself completely from self-condemnation and self-depreciation.

The diversity of Paul's self-image is apparent in his writings. For example, in Romans 7:24 he says, "Wretched man that I am! Who will deliver me from this body of death?" While regarding himself as wretched, he did not measure his true value for himself in these terms. He simply recognized the reality of his human condition. Later on, when his personal situation had probably deteriorated even more, he writes in lofty terms unequaled in the New Testament. Ephesians 1:3 declares, "Blessed be the God and Father of our Lord Jesus Christ, who has blessed us in Christ with every spiritual blessing. . . ."

These words of exultation to the Ephesians were written while Paul was ill and in jail, awaiting execution, and nursing back to health a sick friend who had come to visit him. Obviously he had something to react to other than his own physical circumstances or his status as an educated Jew turned Christian martyr.

Even his successes as a Christian were open to some question. From his jail cell, he wrote to several of his churches admonishing them to refrain from such hideous sins as drunkenness, adultery, incest, pagan worship, and the like. His visible achievements as a church leader would sadden many a bishop's heart. The conclusion has to be that Paul saw himself clearly as an object of the grace of God privileged to do His work. So dominant in his mind was this fact that nothing else really mattered. Not even his sanity was worth protecting in light of who he was as a Christian. (See 2 Cor. 5 and Eph. 1.)

A number of things characterize us who are objects of the love of God. First of all, we are *known people*. Nothing in the mind of any of us is unknown to God. He reads us clearly and completely—better than the most skilled analyst. It is only we who know so little about ourselves. God has far outdistanced us in getting to know us—every well-concealed motive, every latent behavioral tendency, every unresolved conflict, every unsanctified inhibition is clearly understood.

In *The Transparent Self** Professor Sidney Jourard makes the point that it is the unrevealed life that is the troubled

---

*Sidney M. Jourard, *The Transparent Self: Self-Disclosure and Well-Being* (Princeton, N.J.: D. Van Nostrand Company, Inc., 1964), p. 21.

life. The more secretive we are with ourselves, the more protective we need to be; the more deeply hidden are our most treasured sins, the more likely we are to be candidates for emotional and spiritual trouble. To be open to both God and man is to be on the way to healing. Paul makes the point clearly in 2 Corinthians 5:11: "What we are is known to God, and I hope it is known also to your conscience." He hid nothing of himself, even his personal foibles, to those who needed his spiritual nurture.

I remember reading a study of the school records of high-school dropouts in one large city school system. The most significant finding was that these students were largely unknown people. Teachers had trouble recalling their names; their cumulative records in the office were the thinnest and often lacking important information. In the minds of others, they were nobodies, unrevealed people who hid from the world and from others.

In several instances in the New Testament, Jesus is spoken of as revealing Himself to His disciples. I am not sure of the full implication of these references, but I have wondered how well Jesus' disciples knew Him. If Jesus was truly human as we are, was He not also subject to the same need to share Himself with His closest friends? Did He need the same feedback from friends about how He was getting along in life? I suspect He did, and that does not diminish for one moment His full divinity as the Son of God. It simply illustrates how deeply into our lives His redemptive power can go and how it should permeate our Christian fellowship.

The koinonia movement in the church today offers genuine hope for more fully developed lives and more fully operative redemption experiences for all of us. In its best forms, this movement encourages openness and assures us of progress in our growth. Out of it can come deep relationships and mutual understandings that quickly circumvent suspicion and possible breaches in fellowship. By being known men we, too, can affirm, ". . . by the grace of God, I am what I am."

Second, we are ambivalent men. A bundle of mixed-up emotions seems to characterize most of our waking moments. Seldom do we respond to any situation with a clear, pure motive. Competing feelings are our lot. I, for example, enjoy my job, but hate the schedule. I find the people I work with honorable and devoted people—mostly. Some days they would be easier to handle if they weren't such great Christians, then I could clobber them without much misgiving. My wife is a wonderful and charming person, but she's bugging me at the moment about a plumbing problem. My kids are a pleasure, especially when they're asleep. Otherwise they want the car, stay out too late, and think that Sunday School is less than terrific.

Psychologists discovered long ago that love and hate aren't opposite ends of the same pole. In fact, love and hate exist strongly side by side. We often love and hate the same people. Consider troubled marriages, for instance. Every marriage has some ambivalence in it. It's in the marriages ending in divorce that most ambivalence shows up. So intense are the competing emotions that the couple splits up. That takes care of the hate. Now all they have left is the love. So they date each other after the divorce, sometimes sleep together, sometimes even remarry. That gets the hate back. Now they are more mixed up than ever.

How do you feel about your faith? Do you ever have mixed feelings about that? I've known Christians almost strangled in ambivalence about their faith. They know faith is the means of salvation, but they can't seem to shed the guilt they feel. Somebody is always telling them what they aren't and what they ought to be. So they are miserable. Usually that somebody wants everyone to repeat the atonement all over again just for the theological misery of it. To some it just doesn't seem fair that the gift of eternal life is really a gift. So they make themselves miserable trying both to accept the gift and then to repay God for His grace. Nonsense! The gift is free, and loving service is the appropriate response, but not miserable servitude trying to gain spiritual Brownie points to earn one's salvation.

Paul's life was one of ambivalence, too. In Romans 7:15 he writes, "I do not understand my own actions. For I do not do what I want, but I do the very thing I hate." Then he thanks God that in spite of the way he feels and acts, God gives the victory, and as a result there is no condemnation for those who are Christians!

Even Jesus struggled with ambivalence, too. Though we sometimes deny His humanity, the Bible is pretty clear on this point. In fact, at the time that He faced the cross we have perhaps the strongest of all expressions of ambivalence. In Luke 22:42 we hear Him pray, "Father, if thou art willing, remove this cup from me; nevertheless not my will, but thine, be done."

Our most difficult decisions often provoke the greatest ambivalence in us. If we are growing, productive people, our choices are usually between alternatives that are both good and attractive. Therefore to choose one is to let another worthwhile opportunity pass. So often that has been the case as we have decided to move or to stay in one job or location or another. Only with the passing of time and some firm commitment to God has our loss been sustained, even in good moves we have made.

So the first step in handling ambivalence is to recognize that it exists. Don't deny it. No spiritual progress occurs that way. You'll only drive the ambivalent feelings underground, and they will operate anyway in your subconscious mind. Face the fact of mixed emotions. They were known to Paul, as well as to Jesus, and He will go with you and give you the victory you need.

The person apparently without ambivalence is the one

who is in most trouble. Lack of this human conflict is symptomatic of a lack of awareness of some important aspect of one's own experience. Therefore, when genuine mixed emotion stirs us up, it can be a healthy sign. It may mean that we are becoming more sensitive to the real subtleties of a problem that needs our attention. Respect yourself as an ambivalent soul, and know that God cares how you feel.

Third, we are common men. In spite of the fact that much attention is given nowadays to the fact of our uniqueness, we are still all one kind of person, apart from God and without hope except the hope He gives us. If that sounds dire, wait for the rest of the story. It's probably better news than you had imagined.

One of the most misused Bible verses is found in Romans 3:22,23. Usually these verses are quoted to prove the sinfulness of us all and therefore our need for salvation. While this is true about us, it is the secondary premise of this Scripture. The intent of the verse is to cap a discussion Paul has been having with the Romans. He was about to go to Rome for trial and would meet some fellow Christians for the first time. Since he was a Jew and they were Gentiles, he was anxious to point up some similarities between them. So he discussed the fact that since the coming of Christ there is no more advantage to being a Jew. Now they were all the same, just sinners needing a lot of help. "Since all have sinned and fall short of the glory of God." Or so we often quote it, leaving out the first phrase, "For there is no distinction," meaning no difference between Jews and Gentiles.

The point about being a common man is that there is a lot of experience we all know about. Many of our awarenesses are universal. Therefore, when we share ourselves with others it is not as odd an experience as it may seem. There is scarcely a human spiritual need or frustration we know that most others haven't known. Certainly,

152

the cultural differences among people are often great, but we have made so much of this lately that it seems as if we lived in separate worlds entirely. In the common need for relationship with God and each other, little is uncommon. We ought to feel much less reticence in sharing the good news of Jesus Christ. As someone has put it, we are only beggars who have found bread telling other beggars where to find it.

But being a common man means that God knows a lot about us. He once was one of us, too. He was tempted and tried in every way we know, and didn't slip off His throne in the process. We sometimes get the false notion that there are human experiences God doesn't recognize and that therefore He cannot help us in them. But it isn't so. The basis for our fellowship with both man and God is broad and common. The only real differences that count are those between the seekers and the finders, and all of us have been seekers at one time or another.

Paul illustrates his commonness when he declares that he wants to be all things to all men in order to aid in their salvation. It is apparent that he had acquired a great deal of adaptability during the course of his spiritual growth. Once a bitter Jew, spewing hate everywhere, he was transformed into a loving, caring child of God. He was able to be a barbarian to the barbarians, yet argue philosophy with the Greeks on Mars Hill. Using their thought systems and categories, he expounded to them the unknown God and declared Him to be the Christ. In the synagogues and temples, he opened narrow-minded eyes to see the Messiah of prophecy given in the Old Testament. As a Roman citizen, he argued his case before several tribunals, always declaring his faith in Christ.

The common man is an adaptable man, in Christ. I doubt that there is any theory of cultural adaptability anywhere in the psychological literature that accounts for the abilities of Paul. His background was anything but conducive to

153

such flexibility. In fact, rigidity, not flexibility, was the goal of his unconverted mind, for he wanted to make everyone a narrow legalist. His conversion and growth are examples of the possibilities that exist for common men, like you and me. Nowhere in Scripture is there any indication of any limit on what we can become under the grace of God.

So, when God looks at you, what do you think He sees? A common man? A common man, yes, but more. In fact, when God looks at you, do you think He can tell any difference between you and His own Son? I'm not concerned about whether you answer the question yes or no. You may even want to get into a theological argument with me at this point. But if you will study your Bible diligently, I doubt that you'll be able to find any evidence that when God looks at man He sees anyone other than the Son He sent, Jesus. So pull yourself up to your full rights and privileges as a joint-heir with Christ.

The final point I want to make about our identity in Christ, and the most important one, is that we are *righteous men.* You *are* a righteous person—in Christ. Apart from Him, you have no hope. But if you have chosen to be His person and assumed His forgiveness and status, you are entitled to call yourself righteous.

Perhaps that sounds a little presumptuous. I know a number of people who become wary when I suggest this idea to them. They seem to feel that they can call themselves Christians, all right, but they also feel they have to do something, or be something other than what they are, to claim an identity of righteousness. They feel they must gain church status, or spend a few pious years of service, or make some sacrifice before they can attain such an attribute. But the fact is, Christ attributes His righteousness to us and it is not mixed with one whit of our human accomplishment. That's what grace is all about!

In John's Gospel we are told that the function of the Holy Spirit is to convict of sin, of righteousness, and of judgment. Universally guilty man doesn't have too much trouble with the conviction of sin and judgment. He is painfully aware of his problems in this regard. He has been working on his guilt-reduction problems as long as he has been alive, always saying "excuse me," always playing the acceptability games that make one tolerable to society. So to simply assume the identity of righteousness because of the historical act of God seems farfetched and very unconventional.

But the Holy Spirit keeps plugging away at us. He keeps reminding us that there is no righteousness in us on the basis of our own efforts or merits. No amount of "please excuse me for living" will get us anywhere. The same old shortcomings keep dominating our lives, and we get little relief. Oh, once in a while some existential philosopher will come along and smooth things over for an hour or two, but when that reprieve wears off we are back to our old natural state again. But through Christ, the Holy Spirit gives us a gift of assurance that Someone has made up all the differences between what we are and what we ought to be. As a result, we can assume ourselves to be righteous people. And when that fact dawns on us in all of its God-prompted force, a lot of things begin to happen.

I was in the college several years before the reality of this truth got through to me. School had been pretty much of a drag. I had found myriads of friends, lots of intellectual stimulation, and the opportunity to work through many problems, but the real glow of confident life just wasn't there. I suppose I was still achieving my own atonement. I was a Christian, at least in my belief system and behavior, mostly, yet I found it difficult to assume any assurance of genuine freedom in life. But God was at work, chipping away at my assumptions both about Himself and about me. And then one day the truth dawned! I could really be free and assume full status as a righteous person.

This experience came as I was transferring from junior

college to a four-year university. A genuine spiritual awakening had come to the campus, but had missed me completely. I was tired of my efforts to keep things going on the Christian front, and I was not sure of what I should do in life—I had run out of gas spiritually and emotionally. The moment of change came, not in church nor in the stimulus of a great spiritual exercise complete with stereophonic intonations, but on a bright, clear day, when I was home on my parents' farm between school terms. I was feeding the cows, mulling through all my assumptions about life in general, and once more feeling the frustration of my experiences. At that instant, I heaved a pitch fork into the haystack and muttered, "OK, God, you're on! You get whatever is in me, both good and bad."

Changes difficult to describe began to take place. I soon discovered it was all right to be happy. Why inhibit simple joy any longer? I began to lose some of my unsanctified inhibitions. My attitude changed from that of a loser to that of a winner in life. No longer was I willing to accept the put-downs I had felt from those who were still struggling for status. I didn't bother to put them down either, because now I understood the mess they were in. Instead I had a way out of the situation. And I found a lot of people quite willing to listen when they discovered I had received a genuine gift.

Some intellectual changes began to take place, too. My faith had rested at least partly on a fairly airtight, logical, scriptural, orthodox theology. Somehow this seemed necessary to keep God from falling off His throne. I really felt that the right system was important, and it is, but not to keep God on His pedestal. I soon discovered that He has a way of staying put no matter what my intellectual questions may be. As a result, I was able to think through other systems without fear of being done in spiritually. When I hear people haggling about this or that doctrinal insignificance, I wonder if they aren't caught in the web of having to protect God from Christians and themselves from full atonement! But for me, the Bible became an open book, and my relationship to God was affirming, building, and joyous, no longer condemning and wearying.

You *can* safely assume the righteousness of Christ, if you are His. I know of no other grounds for reworking so completely one's self-identity. It will positively change life. Eventually, personal feelings of inferiority and worthlessness will vanish. Fear and a sense of inadequacy will disappear, for it is virtually impossible to hang on to them when one lives continually with the God-given assumption of righteousness!

"From now on, therefore, we regard no one from a human point of view; even though we once regarded Christ from a human point of view, we regard him thus no longer. Therefore, if any one is in Christ, he is a new creation; the old has passed away, behold, the new has come" (2 Cor. 5:16,17).

12 *Mind Changes in Christian Experience*

At one time I served as a consulting psychologist for a Christian ranch attempting to help teen-age boys who were either predelinquent or on probation from the courts. These youngsters had many things in common. Unloved, some had come from homes where there had been little restraint; others from homes where there had been an excessive amount of restraint, even brutality. Uniformly, the boys' morale was low. Many were bitter. They assumed that they were not heirs to a life that mattered; the usual opportunities available to teen-agers could never be theirs. So, what use was there in planning for the future? The boys lived totally for the present moment, often in fear. To endure that moment was oppressive enough—no need to worry about tomorrow's trouble.

The boys refused, too, to discuss such an immediate problem as the remaining months in high school. They failed to see education as a means to an end. To them school was a drag, a pain to be endured. Frequent failure and disappointment blurred time-perceptions. Time was merely a moment crowded with hurt; time was something to be done with, to ignore. Thinking about time became an uncomfortable mental exercise. The more disturbed the

boy, the more he lacked ability to plan ahead, to make reasonable self-predictions about the future. This abnormal attitude in regard to time became a symptom of emotional disturbance.

I became aware of this symptom again when I was teaching a class in child and adolescent psychology. A large class, it had its share of distractable, uneasy students. In the front row sat five disinterested young women, who insisted on smoking during the lecture. They came and went as they pleased during the class hour. But as we progressed through ideas about how normal youngsters grow, as documented by research, their interest picked up remarkably. To their surprise, they discovered that they lived outside the bounds of usual, normal human experience. The most revealing jolt came when we discussed the normal youngster's perception of time and how it changed with growth.

The very young child is frequently confused about the

future. He learns first to differentiate between time periods of the present and the immediate past. Learning to differentiate between the present and the future takes more time. In fact, it takes some youngsters years before they realize that time, apart from their own life, exists at all.

Many ten-year-olds cannot conceive of time as it existed between World War I and World War II. In the same way ancient history is totally incomprehensible to most teen-agers. And accurate prediction of personal experiences as they relate appropriately to plans for the future comes rather late in the high-school years.

The girls in my class learned that their perceptions of time and their ability to plan appropriately for the future had been significantly distorted. Living in a constant uproar and disturbance had given their minds tunnel vision, which focused only on the present. They constantly made planning errors. They had difficulty choosing a major. A couple of them could not readily tell when they were going to be graduated, or if they were. In fact graduation appeared so far away it could not be related to present experiences. These girls deferred making a vocational choice, too. What choices were made often had little bearing on the subjects they studied. Poor timing in these choices led most of them to graduate late, to drop out of school, or to exhaust financial resources before their education was completed.

Yet, their discovery that they deviated from the normal concepts of time opened avenues for discussion. On several occasions we talked about the Christian's dimension of time and eternity and its implications in planning one's life. One of the girls experienced a great deal of emotional healing, which was evidenced in meaningful management of time and planning for the future.

Note one wise man's observation about the matter of time:

"As a child, I crawled and time crawled.

As a toddler, I walked and time walked along.

As a youth, I ran, and time ran, too.
I'm older now, I walk again, but time flies.
Life is done, where has time gone?"

It does seem that the older we grow the more quickly time passes. In fact, now my days fly so fast I frequently question my stewardship of time. How about you? Do you recall elementary school days? Time passed slowly then. You could hardly wait for school to be dismissed. The clock on the wall marked the time—3:35 P.M. You buried your face in your book and read fast and furiously in an effort to hurry the clock. When you thought you could stand it no longer you looked at it again. Do you remember its shout? 3:38!

Now I think that perhaps the ground of experience in perceiving time is shifting. World events occur more quickly. Significant social revolutions come and go several times in a lifetime. Social change that previously occurred slowly now flashes on the screen and off again with such lightning speed that we cannot comprehend it.

I recall the lecture of an anthropologist who had visited an island in the South Seas and observed the customs of its primitive people. Their mode of living and social life style had changed little in hundreds of years. Yet, in the very center of the main village, in an open area created especially for it, sat an American-made freezer in all its glory. The island had no electricity with which to use the appliance, but the invention became a symbol of the dreams of the community. It signaled the fact that as much change could take place in the next forty years as had taken place in the past four hundred.

Our ability to manage our time and our life span indicates the quality of our mental and spiritual lives. The Scriptures admonish: "So teach us to number our days, that we may apply our hearts unto wisdom" (Ps. 90:12). How we manage our time reveals how mature we are.

In my studies I have observed a number of approaches

to the management of time. The first is evidenced in an individual I'll call the *time-grinder*. I once worked with a time-grinder, a man who, knowing he wasn't going to live forever, made every minute count. Sometimes I thought he tried to make some moments count twice. He could be found in his office every morning at seven. He seldom left before seven in the evening. After dinner he either attended school or taught in a local university. By the time he was fifty years old, he had chalked up thirty-two years of experience in public service and had earned two doctoral degrees. He rarely took a vacation. In one seven-year period, he was away from his job only one day. Nothing but exhaustion could deter him.

This may sound like devotion and diligence, and in most people's minds, it was. Yet this man was a highly frustrated person, and those around him who picked up his dissonant vibrations became frustrated, too.

There is also the man who is a *time-killer*. Call him a sluggard if you will. He's like one of my more inept colleagues who always arrived at appointments and meetings fifteen minutes to a half hour early.

"Why?" I asked him one day.

He shrugged. "I just like to kill time, I guess," he said. "Nothing else to do."

This man didn't realize that time is the stuff life is made of. When you kill time, you kill a little of yourself. Life is what's happening while you are making other plans. Time-killing anesthetizes sensitivity to what's happening presently.

It's surprising how many people in the world place no value on the time they have been given. They kill it and go blindly to a disappointing demise.

When I think of the time-killer, I think of a class reunion I emceed several years ago. Twenty-five years had passed since graduation, so we were all eager to see how each person looked and to learn what he had accomplished.

One of our classmates was noticeably absent, however. Because he had been an outstanding student, we were disappointed. Later we learned that fear had kept him from the reunion. He felt that he had done nothing significant with his time and his talents. Guilt-ridden, he dreaded reviewing his life with anyone. Although steadily employed, he had had no real purpose in life and had just gone along killing the clock. Should he ever surmise what he might have been, could he stand the shock?

Now let's consider the *time-preserver.* He's radical in a different sense. He believes that the present moment must be enjoyed, and if possible, retained forever. The past has no value, nor can the future equate with the now.

In his *Study of History** Arnold Toynbee talks of the savior of the time machine, the preserver of the now. Certain civilizations chose this approach as a means to prevent cultural and political demise. Take China as an example. To preserve the present moment for what was once the world's greatest society, this country built walls to prevent any outside influence from penetrating and changing the status quo. The walls became the time machine. *Now,* these people said, will be *forever.* But history has shown that, for hundreds of years, progress was stymied. Only recently has change occurred, and violently, too.

We see examples of time-preservers all around us. The most common are the people who insist on preserving all our institutions in their present form without modification. This is true particularly of our churches, our schools, and their programs. Selfish sacredness is equated with cultural experience that must not be tampered with.

Inability to accept change in institutional life is a symptom of genuine uneasiness about time. A fixation upon a certain time-and-space experience seems necessary to protect oneself from the passing of life. The struggle to

*Arnold J. Toynbee, *A Study of History* (New York: Oxford University Press. 1945), p. 538.

hold onto the good old days results in an attempt to spiritualize present institutions. Their structure, styles, and functions are theologically rationalized. When this happens, those who seek change are forced to become involved in theological battles. But the theological conflict is a charade. The true issue is not theological, but personal and emotional. Unfortunately, many believe the theological rationalizations, and those who seek change begin to question whether or not they have fallen into unbelief. False guilt, which might have been avoided, engulfs both reformer and defender. As a result, progress is impeded and institutions flounder.

Finally, there is the *time-exploiter*. To many of us he is the most recent phenomenon. The rise of existential philosophy in everyday life and among common people has helped promote this approach to the handling of time. Even television commercials advise us to exploit time. You only go once through life, so make your grab while you can and with as much gusto as possible. This is the boobtube's beer-can philosophy, which represents the thought pattern of many people. Enjoy the *now*. Buy *now,* pay *later.* Live it up!

In some instances, individuals have used their inability to reconcile themselves to a proper handling of time as an excuse for riot. History's been a bum steer, they shout. Let's tear up our institutions. Down with tradition. Unseat the establishment. Whatever takes place after the revolution is bound to be better than the present. This clamor for change has come from segments of society, past and present. Again the problem involves deviate living in time. Since eternity is unknowable, or nonexistent, why think about it? In a sense the drug addict says this, too. The present is all there is. So, cop out; lay waste institutions, traditions, and cultures. Do something new. Life is transient at best.

Dr. Theodore W. Anderson, the late president of the

Evangelical Covenant Church, refused to accept this philosophy. In one of his sermons, he said, "I would live as though I had but one day; I would plan as if I had a thousand years." In his own way he paraphrased the Scripture quoted previously: "So teach us to number our days, that we may apply our hearts unto wisdom" (Ps. 90:12).

Because the Christian holds an eternal perspective, he understands this kind of counsel. He knows that all things will be reconciled, in Christ, eventually. Therefore he ought to be more comfortable in the presence of time than anyone else. His life is limitless, his destiny eternal. He is not compelled to settle all issues of the world in his threescore and ten years. He enjoys genuine relaxation, and economy of energy and resource, in the eternal perspective. He knows that nervous tensions need not develop over that which is temporal. When we choose to recondition our emotions with an eternal view of time and institutions, and for that matter, all other things, a lot of our psychosomatic illnesses will subside and the peace of God will reign once more.

The key is the *redemption of time.* As Christians we ought not yield to wasteful resignation in our consideration of time. Neither should we give ourselves to frantic rushing through God's kingdom. Were heaven to move at as hectic a pace as most local churches, it would not be a place of rest. We have much to learn about the appropriate, Christian, gut reaction to time.

Another mind change that occurs with growth involves a change in one's priorities. Different things become important. Certain once-critical questions no longer hold crucial significance. Newly discovered needs come into focus making the adrenalin flow in response to new stimulations.

In a study of priorities, I once tried an interesting experiment. For one week I kept a record of the opening lines of people who came into my office. Almost half of the conversations began with the words, "I know you are busy, but. . . ." As if to say, "I know that your highest priorities do not include me at this time, but if you can spare a minute I'll apologize for bothering you with my problem."

After one such obsequious greeting from a good friend and colleague I replied, "Baloney! I'm not busy, and you're not busy. So why hedge? What's more important than my talking to you right now?" My friend was so stunned he forgot his mission. When he remembered what he came for, he couldn't find words to express himself. We both lapsed into silly laughter every time he tried to talk. You see, we realized to what extent priorities had gone awry. We acknowledged that the many mistaken concepts we hold about what is most important make us feel as though we have to apologize when we want to talk to each other.

Recurrently I find this true. Once I worked in an institution where my office was only a few yards from the office of the chief administrator. But it took two weeks to get an appointment with him. He hibernated for months at a time. When he did open his door, he was so preoccupied with the stack of junk on his desk that he scarcely heard the reason for a subordinate's call. Needless to say, he didn't last many years as an administrator. There were too many broken connections that occurred between people because too much time elapsed between contacts. Delay caused ambiguous dialogue about muddled problems. Relationships were strained and stress heightened by silence. The man didn't know his priorities.

On the other hand, when there is grace in our lives, people become more important than functions. A few years ago I was part of a team of school psychologists who visited several California guidance administrators in search of good innovative ideas. One person we met was head counselor of a large junior high school that was suffering from growing pains. Double sessions, scores of new teachers, and lack of room complicated the guidance program immensely. When we queried the counselor about her role, she clutched a box of registration cards and in a shrill harried voice countered, "As long as I keep track of this, I'm OK! When I don't have this, I'm lost!"

We realized immediately that this woman, and two full-time assistants, were so inundated by growth in their work load that registration cards had become more important than people. They had no time to see anyone. Students became intruders in their lives. They upset the counseling office!

The function of a schedule or of any administrative process is to facilitate relationships among people in the presence of time limits. Yet it is easy to become such a slave to functions and schedules that people get lost in the rush to make time units mesh properly. In our hectic lives of complicated time slots, it is often better to junk the appointment list and just listen to the person at hand.

Nationals in some countries understand this time-priority concept. Our Latin-American neighbors say that time is friendship. Missionary friends tell me that if Africans sense distress in an individual's life, they will come and sit with him. They don't plan to say anything, nor to solve anything. By their presence they just want to convey concern. This is a good example of a proper perspective regarding people, presence, and time. When we learn to put people first in our time allotments, we'll be much more redemptive in our influence. Let God be our guide. He puts people ahead of functions, persons above time slots, life above organizational patterns.

Priorities involve attitudes, too. Under grace, the attitude of affirmation takes precedence over the attitude of negation. The reason for this is soundly biblical. The essential message of God to us is one of hope, love, deliverance, redemption—all attributes of affirmation. Our life is no longer shaped by death, failure, and lack of forgiveness. That's negation and a valid reason why our relationships should be characterized by grace, not by impunity. We affirm people; we do not negate them.

Several years ago I conducted a study of the statements made by junior-high-school teachers to their classes. My colleagues and I found a way to classify each subject and predicate uttered by a teacher in a thirty-minute teaching session. The statements were rated on a five-point scale. A *1*-rating meant that a statement was warm, supportive, and encouraging to the student. A *5*-rating meant the statement was hostile, punitive, or discouraging to the student. A *3*-rating classified statements of neutral character, usually made in explanation of a lesson. Ratings of *2* and *4* represented intermediate values on the scale. A *2* indicated a moderately supportive statement; a *4*, a moderately unsupportive statement.

We were pleased to find that most teachers were more often warm than they were hostile. Perhaps this speaks well of the teaching profession. In another test we measured the relative degree of anxiety and tranquility experienced by students. The results confirmed what we had believed to be true. When teachers were hostile and unsupportive, anxiety rose. When they were supportive and friendly, anxiety diminished.

In this same experiment, we also asked principals to rate their teachers according to the quality of teaching they believed prevailed. Again, affirming teachers rated higher than those who were inclined to be negative.

One might ask if it is possible for a person to change attitudes of this kind. Yes, it is. Benjamin Franklin is supposed to have claimed that he changed from a curmudgeon to an affable gentleman by consciously changing the nature of his responses to people. Through this action his acceptance by others improved. So it can be with us. When we choose to affirm people, they respond affirmatively to us. When we are punitive, we drive men away. Recall that Jesus attracted a motley assortment of men around Him.

Winebibbers and gluttons ate with Him. The poor received friendship and help. The sick flocked to Him. These people were recipients of the affirmation and redemption that He allowed to flow from Him. Like Christ, let us affirm and love people; let us put impunity aside. Redeemed people lose their need to punish. They are not driven to correct every visible sin. Instead they earn the love of men who, because of affirmation, choose to sin no more.

Another change in priority involves a change in relationship with God. If we choose the best, we enter into a first-name relationship that is more personal, less abstract, less theologically burdened.

I've often noticed how, when some people pray, they seem unable to talk to God without first repeating long theological affirmations that He exists, exists in three persons, lives in heaven, has become incarnate in human flesh, has pretty well established his superiority over angels, earthquakes, demons, and the fate of the human race. I don't know who is supposed to be impressed, but I wonder if God doesn't chuckle when He listens to such discourse from the mouths of His saints. How would you like to have someone establish your ancestry, address, attributes, past history, and role in society before he says, "Hello!"

To be personal does not mean we are disrespectful. On the contrary it means that we show our respect more fully in a personal relationship. To be personal implies a state of openness and a vulnerability to one another. In an open relationship, respect is felt more keenly than an insult would be. So the fact that one uses personal terms in conversation does not, in and of itself, evidence disrespect. Rather it is one's conduct, when it is personal, that matters.

Many people have trouble being personal with God. They have been conditioned to experience Him only in worshipful awe. Or they have known Him only in great theological contexts which, to the human mind, seem incompatible with personal relationships. But one need not

170

assume such an attitude. God can be experienced both personally and worshipfully. One type of expression does not preclude the other, nor does it prove which is spiritually superior.

The personal relationship implies a sense of safety. We are personal only with those in whose presence we feel safe. When we feel threatened, we become impersonal. The reduction of threat between people immediately creates a personal feeling of confidence and safety. But many people can't think beyond the concept that it is a fearful thing to fall into the hands of the living God. They do not sense that there is safety in Christ because He removed threat from life.

Such people need wiggle room. They must be able to approach and withdraw without feeling they demean themselves in God's sight. This is how we try any new experience. We move in, back away, get close again, then retreat. There is nothing wrong in so doing as long as we persist and actually do draw near to God.

When we are personal with God, we give Him more of our lives. When we live close to Him, the spectrum of our concerns widens immediately. Our prayers include both small and great affairs. The most remote problem, or the least significant problem in our eyes, receives His attention. We become full-spectrum Christians for whom no human factor is exempt from grace.

When we think of God as impersonal, we tend to equate Him with abstractions, forces in the universe, unalterable causes. It seems impossible that the mind of God can change because we carry on a personal conversation with Him. Yet because His mind does seem to change, we find we are entitled to believe that the hand of God does move when we pray.

One of the great joys I have found in my Christian life is the freedom to perceive an ever-widening array of human experiences. I say this because my growth as a Christian has been accompanied by an increase in my feelings of fear. Let me explain. The increased fearfulness has developed as I have continued my work in professional psychology. I have done many case studies of young people who have had all sorts of problems. The recommendations I made, after thorough evaluation of all factors, resulted in actions that placed some children in institutions, extended their prison sentences, removed them from their homes, assigned them to classes for the retarded, and gave others enriched school opportunities. There was a time when this responsibility did not perturb me to any great extent. That is no longer true. It is not that such actions have been particularly bad, often they have been good. It's just that I understand more fully how these people must have felt about the changes wrought in their lives because of my work.

Once a ministerial board asked me to test a clergyman who was having serious difficulties in the ministry. Unable to relate to any kind of authority himself, he expected his church members to submit unquestionably to his will. This inconsistency, accompanied by a moral lapse, made him impossible to deal with. As a result of my study, in which he had been very uncooperative, I recommended that his license as a minister be revoked. In this instance, my recommendation was not accepted by him or by the board members who had requested the study. He was permitted to continue his work, which eventually almost destroyed his congregation.

I recall how I fought my emotions as I wrote that final recommendation. I realized how my action would affect his wife and family; it shook me to the core. There had been a day when I would not have been moved by such involvement. However, my growth as a Christian made it a more difficult task. I had become more afraid, not less. I sensed the tragedy more keenly. I suspect that the ruling members of the licensing board could not, because of their sensitivity, bring themselves to accept the recommendation. It hurt them, too. Yet, because they ducked the immediate pain, they had to face a more serious backlash.

The truth remains, however, that as we grow, we hurt more, we fear more, we experience more. We become sensitive, more vulnerable, more acquainted with the sorrows and griefs of other men.

Do you recall that I began this line of thought by saying that it was a joy to perceive an ever-widening array of human experience? But how can increased fear be joyous? Am I inconsistent in my arguments? It seems so, I know. Yet such perception is joyous—not in some ascetic sense, either. As we learn to perceive more of life and feel needs more keenly, we become more realistic, more reality oriented. It is a fundamental truth that reality, and the accurate perception of it, is therapeutic even if it does hurt. This is because as we perceive more fully, we are also able to experience our joys more fully. And for Christians, there is much more joy than sorrow. This must be what Paul meant when he told us to count it joy when we find ourselves in tribulation. If Paul hadn't proved that he believed this, he would long ago have been chalked off as a masochistic nut, or at least as a foolish ascetic who got big kicks out of pain.

And what about experiences that affect the entire universe? Isn't it surprising that God has entrusted to us the solutions to these pressing problems—matters like the population explosion, worldwide pollution, transplants of organs, and altered genetic structures? I find it amazing that the Bible is more silent than vocal about these matters. Oh, I know that some individuals insist that the Bible gives precise direction regarding them, but really, much is left for us to figure out. Have you ever wrestled with the theology of organ transplants, for instance? When science finds a way to preserve your gifted, experienced, well-adjusted brain and to place it in the body of a person thirty years younger than you, whose soul becomes whose? Who goes to heaven? You or the recipient of your mind? Work on that for awhile and when you figure it out, write me and tell me what your answer is. If you are driven up a wall because you can't come up with an answer and aren't able to chuckle about it, I'll say your salvation is missing an important ingredient—the ability to experience joy in a dilemma.

Some people can't afford to be joyful. They are so busy guarding themselves against hurt while working out their salvation that they forget that joy is part of the Christian experience. If they felt joy, they would also feel hurt, and then they might lose their cool. How about you? Do you find it better to be miserable than to lose your cool? Think again. Maybe your cool is preventing an experience of grace. You might consider letting God have your cool, too.

I knew a college dean who was known for his unemotional approach to every problem. Nothing bothered or upset him. But nothing made him happy, either. To him hilarity involved nothing more than a slight quiver of the upper lip; extreme sadness, a slight quiver of the lower lip. Poor Dr. Cool! He never knew what a good emotional airing meant, nor did he know the warmth of close personal friendships. He lived and died alone.

I'm glad I've found joy in the long straight flight of a golf ball; in the smile of a daughter who just beat her best backstroke record in the local pool; in a cool evening breeze as I sit on the back steps of my home.

At present I'm trying to find joy in winds whipping off Lake Michigan. Maybe I'll make it. I'm also trying to find joy in running out of gas on the expressway at rush hour in 98 degree temperature and 99 percent humidity in downtown Chicago. Maybe I'll learn that, too. But I'm not sure I want to. It's that old problem of ambivalence again. I only know life is a lot richer when I open my emotions to God who is involved in everything.

Emotional constriction is a symptom of generalized hang-ups in life. When we feel neither joy nor pain, we are in danger. It is the unmoved soul who is headed for trouble, not the one who feels a wide range of experiences. If we work hard to contain a single emotional experience, chances are we will constrict a lot of other feelings, too. But when we fearlessly let God in on all of our feelings, He redeems us and sets us free—free to sense all that, in His omniscience He has provided for us.

13 *A Case in Point*

Not long ago I learned to know a man by reading the record of his life. Though he lived in another time and in another part of the world, his personal story illustrates most of the ideas presented thus far. As I tell you his history, try to put yourself in his shoes. See if you can feel as he must have felt.

I first discovered him as a middle-aged man. It's that time of life when one makes many personal assessments. I'm middle-aged myself so I can identify quite readily with our friend's experience. We tend to aggrandize our experiences as we grow older. We subtly add significance to things we have done. We forget our failures. Our sterling qualities emerge virtually without blemish.

But the friend of whom I speak had occasion to be a realist. In middle age he suffered from reasonably severe physical handicaps. His vision was impaired, possibly because of an epileptic or diabetic condition. We are not at all sure of this, but we recall there were problems of loss of consciousness associated with poor eyesight. Naturally this presented problems. Being alone and having to communicate through writing must have been very difficult. Imagine his frustration trying to find someone who would take a few minutes to read his mail for him! He was in jail at the time. And the outlook was grim. Further, the literacy rate was low where he was confined, and it is doubtful that many of his keepers could or would honor his literary requests.

Our friend was a man of letters. He had studied in the outstanding schools of his day. An excellent student, he had majored in history and theology. His academic reputation was well known. In fact, his perceptive writings were regarded as treasures and passed from group to group so that many could profit from his ideas.

But he was a peculiar man, peculiar in the sense that he acted on his beliefs. In this he was different from us. We aren't quite so involved with what we know. More often we stumble over some truth and get up and go on as though nothing ever happened. Not so our friend. Something propelled him to act upon what he learned. When his ideas changed, his actions changed. And people were startled by his altered behavior. He might well have borne the radical label had he lived in the contemporary scene.

As a result of his profound commitment to ideas, he became a leader among men. At a young age, his church conferred on him leadership roles often reserved for men many years his senior. And while young, he was elected to the highest authoritative body of his religious order. In some ways it seemed that he was an eccentric, single of mind and purpose—a zealot in the true sense of the word.

We know little of his early history and background. We know nothing about his relationships to parents or about early successes and traumas. We can only guess what his childhood was like. It would seem that the personality he developed could have used some help. As a young adult, he acted like a hostile religious intellectual. People held

178

him both in esteem and in fear. We find no sense of loving closeness from descriptions we have of him. When he writes about himself, he avoids all reference to early childhood and youth. I suspect that he was deprived of a great deal of early healthy emotional care. This dearth of information about his childhood may be significant in view of what happened later.

Often the hostile intellectual becomes a leader. It is strange, but sometimes emotional illness entices men more than health does. How many times have you seen a religious leader with a burr in his saddle and a message of stress on his heart win large followings wherever he goes? It happens over and over again, and our friend may have been one who exercised these psychological propellents. In fact, so punitive had his personality become that he often sought legal redress in the courts for those who opposed him. Often they were cast into prison. Even death sentences were meted out to his adversaries in the name of the Kingdom of God. One wonders how long this could go on without conflicts building in his mind and perplexing his soul.

Then at the very height of his punitive religious career, he experienced an about-face. A blinding, mind-blowing, ego-assaulting jolt discomposed him. The latent conflict that had been brewing now burst upon him with tempest fury. And he changed as few men have been known to change. Both his followers and his victims were astounded. No one could comprehend what had happened. Nor did anyone know how to deal with him. Incomprehensible as it was, the public was forced to wrestle with the change. Now the man loved his enemies. They, in turn, felt he should be accepted, though they still feared him. On the other hand his friends ostracized him. He no longer carried out the repugnant orders of his sect. Instead he disappeared from view for several months, no doubt in an effort to collect his own thoughts.

179

However, regardless of circumstances, no man with leadership aptitude loses his ability to gather a following. In his change, this man had lost none of this latent talent. But now his zeal was redirected. Genuine love had replaced hostility. New relationships began to develop for new reasons. Everywhere he went people listened to his story. Some argued with him. They provoked him in any way they could to test the validity of his experience. But his character was firm. He could not be shaken.

In time, a number of groups formed that were sympathetic to his teachings. These people adopted his new life style as theirs. His new-found zeal became the incentive that caused him to travel to all the great trade centers of the world. Here his ideas were challenged in every marketplace of thought.

Later a time of disappointment set in. Some of his followers fell into moral disrepute. His teachings became an excuse for the grossest immoralities, sexual deviance and lust. Besides, there arose a group who challenged his authority and his logic. Jealous peers tried desperately to discredit him. They wanted to appropriate some of his popularity for themselves. Eventually nearly all of the groups that fanned around him disintegrated, never to be heard from again, except in written epitaphs.

The legal principles in his part of the world were quite different from ours. We say a man is innocent until proved guilty. But where he lived, men were presumed guilty until proven innocent. Such was the case in this man's life. His ideas finally caught the attention of civil authority. So much clamor arose when he taught that public disturbances were common. The authorities finally decided that something had to be done to curb these outbreaks. Consequently he was brought to trial on several occasions. The first trials were generally insignificant. He was regarded as an odd one who really did nothing wrong—it was just the manner in which he went about it. So cool it, admonished the counselors of the law! But cool it, he could not. He just wasn't made that way!

Trial followed trial, usually in a sequence of appeals to higher courts. Finally a conviction from the highest court was obtained. He must die for his crime.

So we find him at middle age—convicted and sentenced to die. With his followers in disrepute for their immorality, his personal career could be regarded by most as shipwrecked. No assets accumulated. No retirement plans made. No family that cared. Little visible impact made on the society in which he lived. What now?

Are you able to identify with our friend? How would you feel if this were your situation? Another thought—how would you explain the tremendous change that had taken place in his life—a change that made a loving shepherd out of a hostile zealot?

These are not farfetched considerations. At middle age you have either obtained an education, or you have not. You have successfully married and raised a family, or you have not. You have achieved some stability of career, or you have not. You have achieved early aspirations, or you have settled for less. The opportunities have diminished with the years, and now there is no turning back.

It isn't surprising that many people become depressed at this stage of life. At least one researcher of my acquaintance claims that beginning middle age—from about forty to fifty—is the age of maximum mental depression. Most of the dreams that might have been probably will never be realized. This is the age of the man we have described. How does he feel? In a very real sense, it is difficult to empathize fully with him. Most of us do not have a death sentence hanging over us, so our condition is not so acute as his. Nevertheless, I challenge you to put yourself emotionally in his place.

We are fortunate in that we do have a record of our friend's feeling at this moment. We can read about it simply by turning to chapter 1 of the book of Ephesians in the New Testament. Listen to these words in verses 3 and 4. "Blessed be the God and Father of our Lord Jesus Christ, who hath blessed us with all spiritual blessings in heavenly places in Christ: According as he hath chosen us in him before the foundation of the world, that we should be holy and without blame before him in love."

Depressing words? Far from it!

I'm sure you recognize that what you have been reading is a nonspiritual interpretation of the life of the apostle Paul, before and after his conversion. The verses quoted represent the loftiest emotional expression of Paul anywhere in the New Testament.

This passage creates a problem for the serious student, however. How can a man react with such elation having come through a turbulent life such as his? Here he was, awaiting his doom, reviewing a life of personal failure, with no family that cared. The Bible does record that one friend visited him in prison. But he got sick. In fact the visitor, Epaphroditus, became so ill that Paul feared he would not live. Fortunately he recovered, but such illness could scarcely have contributed much elation to the moment!

It would be normal procedure for a psychologist to question Paul's reaction to the whole situation. Was he in his right mind? Can a sane man exult under such stress? Normally we expect people's emotional reactions to match their experiences. When they do not match, but seem too much out of character, we presume some serious distortion of thought process has occurred. In Paul's case we must face the fact that either he was seriously misperceiving as a result of his stress or something most unusual had happened to change the emotional dynamics of his life. Can we assume that the earlier dramatic change in his life had something to do with it?

Having considered this question regarding Paul's ability

to rejoice under stress, a friend of mine, a psychiatrist, simply says that Paul was a schizophrenic whose reactions had so departed from reality that he was experiencing emotional delusions. No sane man would react to such dire circumstances with such elation.

What do you think? Are there other clues to the problem? Was Paul's experience potentially so renewing and transforming that all the psychological rules of human emotional reaction must be reviewed? Is there a personality dynamic in force in the lives of Christians, but not in others? Perhaps Paul gives us a clue in other writings.

In all Paul's writings, one chapter of Scripture gives particular insight into the psychological workings of the conversion experience. The passage is found in 2 Corinthians 5. Beginning with verse 11, note the statements from which we can derive principles about the converted personality.

Paul had no loss of reality about his life situation. He talks of it freely and openly. In chapter 4 he pulls no punches about feeling uncomfortableness in his experience. For example, verses 8 and 9 say: "We are troubled on every side, yet not distressed; we are perplexed, but not in despair; persecuted, but not forsaken; cast down, but not destroyed."

The fact that Paul clearly perceived reality precludes any real notion that he was not in his right mind. This was no schizophrenic experiencing delusions of grandeur or persecution. This was a man with his full wits about him, never denying his suffering, but so taken with God's promises that suffering was of little consequence to him. In fact, a casual reading of the entire book of 2 Corinthians underscores this truth. He had a better grip on reality than most Christians. As a result he could vindicate both his apostleship and his enthusiasm while encouraging the faltering Corinthian Christians.

Back to chapter 5. In verses 11 and 12, Paul deals with the the first of several psychological principles. The first is the principle of identity—finding out who you are, finding out who you are in the full context of the love and judgment of God.

In chapter 4, we talked about the need to see oneself as an adequate person. This is what identity is all about. When we come to see ourselves as the objects of God's unmerited love and pull ourselves up to that full image, we have established the most important basis for seeing ourselves as adequate persons. When we respond in faithful service, without much regard to whether our service is humanly regarded as worthwhile achievement or not, we establish the other most important basis for identity. Accepting the love of God makes us realize that we are worthwhile. No inferiorities are permitted here. If God thinks you are somebody, you are somebody, no matter what society has to say about it. When you respond in faithful service, you meet every expectation of God. He wants you to serve, not to achieve as men commonly understand achievement in an economic, status-conscious world.

Paul then contrasts this identity with the identity obtained by others. In verse 12, he speaks about those who feel that achievement is better than service, or status better than the nature of one's heart. Apparently there were those who still thought they could earn enough Brownie points to make themselves acceptable to God. No way! You must start where you are, be what you are, let God make up all the differences, and then in love serve Him.

Paul says, "By the grace of God, I am what I am" (1 Cor. 15:10). When you are God's nothing else really matters! Your identity is cast in the simple fact that you are the object of boundless love, regardless of any human assessment.

The second principle of the Christian psychological life that Paul deals with is the principle of nonownership of self. This is the principle that is likely to be hotly contested by theorists of personality. Ours is the day when it is a great thing to be one's own person. In various ways you have heard men say, "I want to be my own man!" The courts attempt to balance individual rights with the rights of society, a balance that needs periodic reexamination. Education sets as its goal the development of the individual so that he can obtain a state of psychological autonomy. Political scientists assume that all nations have the right to determine their own destinies.

But Paul is of another mind. He assumes that it is better to be dead to oneself, not to live for oneself. To be dead to oneself is to cease owning oneself. And it is no secret that we become pretty much wrapped up in what we own.

185

This is true whether we own property, children or position. Conversely, we lose involvement when ownership ceases. I no longer worry about the heater in the house I sold a couple of years ago. I don't get excited if the neighbor's window breaks in a windstorm, though I might help him fix it. I feel far less deeply about the welfare of other people's children than I do about my own. So what might happen if I ceased ownership of myself? Suppose I could give up ownership of my fears, my talents, my concerns about health. Would that help?

Apparently Paul had been able to transfer title of himself to God. In fact, the effect of his words is to say, "So what if I'm crazy? That's God's business. So what if I'm sane? Then I can live for you." (See verse 13. The Amplified New Testament has an especially good treatment of the passage.) Apparently Paul had given up even the ownership of his own sanity. Ah, sanity, that most prized of men's possessions! What struggles a man will endure so as not to lose his mind!

But if a man does not own even his own sanity, doesn't it stand to reason that he'll be a lot less self-involved? Won't he worry a lot less about how he appears to others? Shouldn't he be able to stop about half his struggle with life? Wouldn't a lot of psychotherapy be cut short if the object of that therapy were suddenly unimportant, or at least of secondary value?

Some years ago I counseled with a young man who was just beginning the ministry. Problems of depression beset him to the extent that he could not continue his service to his church. The climax came when in the middle of a sermon he began to weep. Unable to control himself, he closed the service and ran home. He believed his life had ended.

His loss of occupation greatly multiplied his problem. Now he was unable to support his family. As a result he lost much self-esteem. His wife went to work as a secretary and kept the family going for almost a year. Needless to say, the depressive episodes increased, and he considered institutionalizing himself. Before many weeks had passed, he refused even to go outside his home, fearing what friends and neighbors would say.

As we began to converse about the problem, I learned that success and the esteem of parishioners were critically important to this man. He was well educated in the Christian faith and frequently preached on successful Christian living, but now his message was fading rapidly. In his darkest moments he considered suicide as a way out. But this would not do either. What about those victorious messages? What about the family? He was afraid to live and afraid to die.

Depression is often a mask for deep hostility, and as we counseled it became apparent that this man was unconsciously hiding a lot of anger. Apparently one of his motives for going into the ministry was to prove himself worthy to both God and man, particularly to a very spiritual father who had demonstrated little approval of his son. Since neither God nor his dad seemed pleased by the young minister's efforts, the result was murky depression.

After much venting of hostility and verbalizing about his relationship to his father, he felt relieved. Yet he still did not know what to do next. "If I could only feel free to go crazy," he muttered one evening as we talked, "I think half the battle would be over."

"Why don't you see if you can," I suggested.

"That sounds as crazy as I do," he retorted, "but it makes a silly kind of sense!" At this point we entered into some meaningful discussion of what it means to be owned by a God who is utterly in charge of our affairs, a God who cares deeply and one to whom we can fully abandon ourselves. Then we talked about Paul in 2 Corinthians. Was his principle of self-abandonment really a valid one?

In succeeding sessions, this young man began yielding

ownership of himself. Yielding meant also surrendering his problems and emotions. One doesn't give God only the nice-looking things inside the head. He gives all. When my friend did this in sweet release and abandonment, half the battle was won. Since he was now acceptable to God, he no longer needed to please an over-expecting dad.

Bit by bit, health returned. A call to a new charge came, and he was able to respond with genuine enthusiasm. Today he has a freedom and sensitivity to people known by few Christians. He is not his own, he has been taken over by God. Paul writes in 1 Corinthians 6:19,20, "Ye are not your own, for ye are bought with a price: therefore glorify God in your body, and in your spirit, which are God's."

If the two principles we have stated are true, then a whole new theory of personality must emerge. If it is true that identity can be gained simply by replacing the usual efforts at attaining a good self-image with the recognition that God loves us, then hope is available for untold numbers of people. Every major theory of personality in today's textbooks regards identity as some kind of achievement, and almost never as a gift. Secular theorists cannot conceive of the idea that "by the grace of God I am what I am."

Further, if it is true that one can relinquish self-ownership thus reducing markedly self-anxieties, then current psychotherapy must be reevaluated. Most anxiety reduction for therapy clients is obtained by accomplishing something, never by giving something away.

The implication for current personality theory is that the Christian can postulate a theory that does not have human ego at its center. Instead of being in nuclear position, the ego of man is orbital in the organization of himself. So far this idea is unheard of in today's psychology systems. Virtually every sophisticated theory of human personality supposes that man was made with ego as the central fact of the human life. The goal of all development of the person is to see that this ego is protected, fulfilled, enhanced and valued. But Paul says no. Instead the Christian must come to understand that God is nuclear in human personality and ego is orbital. Thus the Christian view contradicts most of what is known in the psychological theories of man.

God is not just an idea. He is not just a concept to be used to cover the unexplainable. Nor is Christian faith an alternative among alternatives. It is not a system alongside other systems—an idea that can readily be accepted or rejected without consequence. Rather, how one deals with the God of the Bible and the Christ who is His Son has vital implication for the very structure of one's personal and emotional life.

In most psychological theory, the goal of existence is to experience an integrated wholeness with ego at the center of life. Therefore mental health and emotional well-being become all-important. But not so with the Christian. For him, his faith is not just a means of achieving a state of mental well-being to be discarded when that function is not fulfilled. Instead, mental health and emotional well-being are by-products of an experience wherein God is nuclear in life, ego is orbital, and the purpose of living is giving honor and praise to God, who alone is capable of receiving such adoration. If in turn, God gives one mental wholeness, well and good; but it is not first in God's spiritual and mental economy.

The pursuit of mental health is a secondary effect of a yielded life. In fact, pursuing it as an end in itself only reinforces the ego centrality of most people's experience. When well-being comes as a by-product, it comes in greater simplicity, in greater quantity, and in total harmony with the ultimate purpose of man.

If we trust God and seek to bring honor to Him, the problem of peace of soul will largely take care of itself. In 1 Corinthians 2:9 Paul says: "What no man ever saw

189

or heard, what no man ever thought could happen, is the very thing God prepared for those who love him." Further, in Philippians 4:6,7 he says (and this is my own paraphrase), "Don't worry about anything, pray about everything, give thanks for anything, and the peace of God, which exceeds all human ability to understand, will take care of both your mind and your emotions through Christ Jesus."

When Jesus was about to leave this earth He gave a similar promise to His disciples. It is found in John 14:27. "Peace I leave with you, my peace I give unto you: not as the world giveth, give I unto you. Let not your heart be troubled, neither let it be afraid."

14 The Need for Worship

Most people think of worship as a religious phenomenon without implication for psychological life. It has been viewed by many as one of those things religious people do for no rational reason except that the church seemed to get started on it and couldn't let it go. It is seen as an esoteric and quaint religious exercise with only symbolic meanings. Most people are right. It is an esoteric happening without much sense unless the fact of genuine conversion has taken place. Then the dynamics change altogether. Once God moves in, perspectives on what is real or rich and what is esoteric or meaningless do an about-face.

My attention was firmly fixed upon this matter a number of years ago when A. W. Tozer, writing in a magazine article, pointed up the fact that most people today have lost the concept of the Shekinah glory of God radiating through temple worship. Christians have become introspective to the point that all religious experience is ego involved, internal in the soul, and judged by what I get out of it. Any Christian experience that does not focus upon some personal need has been effectively eliminated but this is not the nature of worship.

About the same time I was pondering the fact that

191

worship and related religious experience is one of the few universal forms of behavior. The worship of God in some form is present nearly everywhere in the world. Every culture has it, except the highly educated culture. It is in this culture alone that atheism thrives. One of the unfortunate aspects of human educational progress is the cessation of worship by sophisticated people. Actually, cessation is concerned only with the religious elements of worship. The human being secularized by learning still worships; he has only switched objects. Man may think that he has advanced his understanding enough to eliminate the necessity of religious experience but he is only deceived. Worship is still with him even though forms have changed and objects replaced. Man can no more live without worship than he can live without love.

My awareness of the need for worship was further heightened by noting the great prayers of Scripture. There are four prayers commonly regarded as the great petitions of the Bible. The first is David's prayer when he was refused the privilege of building the Temple. Too much blood was shed in his time, and God reserved the right of building the Temple for Solomon, David's successor. David seems disappointed but, nevertheless, accepts the injunction of God. His response is not one of introspective soul searching as much as one of a great worship experience. He honors God for who He is, puts aside his self concerns, and proceeds to collect the materials neceessary for temple construction at a later date.

David was able to set aside pampering his own emotions and utter the phrases that describe the greatness and holiness of God. In a time of stress, David points upward rather than inward. There is no great analysis of his own spiritual condition to explain why God had acted in His sovereign way.

Solomon later was granted the right to build the great edifice that evoked awe in every beholder. The description of the temple in the Old Testament sends the calculators of the mind whirling. The expense was fantastic, the designs magnificent. When dedicated, thousands of voices in united choir appeared twenty-four hours a day as part of the dedication ceremony. In the midst of the celebration, Solomon prays. And his prayer is a model of worshipful experience. All the majesty and grandeur of God is acclaimed. In hearing the prayer, no mind could miss the priorities for spiritual experience that were apparent. No building committees were congratulated, no slaves who cut timbers or mined gold were named, no heartfelt thanks for the pledges of the church membership were mentioned. Instead the Shekinah glory of God was clearly set forth in a way that only the most obtuse observer would miss.

Likewise, in both the great prayers of Jesus the worship elements are present. "Our father who art in heaven, hallowed be thy name. . . ." No immediate mention of human introspective experience is made. It does come later, but it is not first. First the glory of God. First the recognition of who is sovereign. First the declaration of who God is.

I have come to recognize these prayers as models of Christian mental experience. The Christian mind must be so programmed that the immediate response to all human experience is a response of worship. Whether that experience is one of joy or sorrow, it matters not. Worship is the modus operandi of the mature spiritual mind.

Such a mind existed in Job. You may recall that Job received, with the permission of God, one of the most severe tests of character. He was plagued with the loss of livestock, the loss of sons, and the loss of health. Grief was his lot in overwhelming measure. His personal losses were so great that even his wife could not sustain them. "Curse God and die" was her encouragement. Three friends of Job picked up the chant as well.

What did you do at your most grievous moment? What advice did you get? The inquisition that Job's friends conducted may have been more troublesome than his losses. His losses obviously did not sway him from his worshipful commitment to God. Nor did loss even suggest such a response. His friends did. Obviously Job was guilty of something and they advised a spiritual self-search into every gloomy cavern of his mind. What fun that might have been. But Job was not so disposed. Instead, he stripped himself of all other symbols of status and wealth and entered into worship. In sackcloth and ashes, with heart and mind bare before God, he declares that though God slay him, yet will he trust. Neither would he enter into personal introspection to falsely identify guilt when there was none. Instead, worship was his response!

Since I regard worship as the fundamental frame of mind for the Christian and as the modus operandi of mature spiritual experience, I want to advance five propositional statements concerning the psychological nature of worship.

First, you will worship something. Whether you are Christian, heathen, atheist, or syncretist, or of any other persuasion, you will worship something. At some point in your life you will give yourself to something. It may not be an altogether conscious experience, but you will give yourself to something. And whatever claims you will be your object of worship.

Earlier in the book we talked about the nature of agape love, a love that is given without merit on the part of the receiver. It is unearned. Similarly, you will set up something as a recipient of your attention and devotion. You will make a conscious or an unconscious commitment of your life to something, some cause, some purpose, some person, or some combination of all of these and never mind the validity of the object or its worthiness. Something will occupy the center of your life and claim your devotion even if that claim seems to occur by default.

The apostle Paul points out that people set up agape relationships with all kinds of unworthy objects. Men may decide that they are economic creatures and spend virtually all of their lives in economic pursuits. Many are successful and die known as the richest men in the cemetery. But you don't have to be rich to worship money. Sometimes being poor calls so much attention to money that poor men worship the not-so-almighty buck. An unmerited object is chosen for an unfortunately overrated relationship.

It is easy to demonstrate that money is not worth the worship it gets. Testimonials exist all around us to this effect. People observe the evidence and hope to do better. So the search for objects to worship is incessantly pursued. Several alternatives have been found and today are claiming the devotion of many.

In one of my classes in human growth and development I raised the question about valuable reasons for living. "Why grow up, anyway," I chided. "What's the reason?" A middle-aged gentleman who had returned to college to "find himself" was hooked by the question. It made him restless and uncomfortable because he had no real answer, yet he knew it was the most important issue he faced. He saw his life running out without purpose, and without this he knew he faced a most unpleasant demise. Strange isn't it that the people with the least reason to live have the hardest time dying! Unfortunately, this gentleman decided that the only alternative left to him was the devotion of all his resources to existential experience. He would seek to make meaning out of life by consuming himself in sensory experience and the exhaustion of his resources in a wide range of mind-blowing episodes. So he chose to worship the exploration of his sensual life. He could hardly have taken a wilder ride to hell. He knew full well what was in store, but he was fresh out of alternatives. He felt nothing was worth anything so why worry about the value of anything. And blow his mind he did—all in the search for something to abate his need for an object of worship.

Unfortunately this man represents a trend overtaking thousands of young people. The worship of economic success, the history of warfare in man, the injustices of the world—all have left man without alternatives. The worship of sensory or even illusory experience is a dominant trend, not because it represents so great an alternative, but simply because so many other things have been tried and found wanting.

Yet another object of worship is political system and ideology. The rational and objective merits of these systems certainly don't explain the devotion attached to them. They are as hollow and unfulfilling as any of man's futile experiences. But what most people don't recognize is that the merits of the object of their devotion matters little. A person must be devoted to something. He must worship or he will disintegrate! So the best of a poor lot of alternatives is chosen. An ideology or political system with even the remotest possibility of improving matters is going to be chosen by many.

In a similar way people yearn to devote themselves to anything that promises power over people and events. I am both amused and alarmed by the tremendous impact of behavioral psychology these days. B. F. Skinner's book *Walden Two* set off nationwide, even worldwide discussion of a theory that promised to make events controllable and predictable. Interestingly enough, the principles involved in the psychological system underlying *Walden Two* work rather well in quite a number of situations. I have personally seen undisciplined classes of disturbed children brought under control by the operant conditioning techniques suggested in behavioral psychology. Obstreperous behavior has been abated, teachers' anxiety reduced, and praises to Skinner—hallelujah! Extrapolate the principles and you have a world under control. This is not too different from what the Marxists are telling the world. They say man is a product of his conditioning and by consciously

196

manipulating him you can make of him what you will—presumably an equalitarian social animal where only productive motives prevail.

But then Nietzsche had similar ideas and so did Rousseau, Hegel, Aristotle and Plato. Plato thought that if all men would turn seriously to philosophy, human events would be both controllable and predictable. Thus the philosophers have had incessant following down through the ages, not so much because their points were either valid or invalid, but because men needed something to worship—something to command total devotion.

The second premise is that without worship, life disintegrates. Some object of worship must be present to organize the human personality. It is a matter of secondary importance, psychologically, whether or not the worship object is valid. There must be a something around which to bind and build all of life. Something besides self must be in the middle of things. While men seem to build life around themselves, what they are unconsciously doing is

197

seeking a replacement for their ego-centered experiences. The need for worship explains this impulse to replacement.

My interpretation of both Bertrand Russell and Jean Paul Sartre is that both had run so far out of options for objects or worship they turned to despair as the organizing point of human experience. Life had to be built out of the firm ground of despair, since neither had found anything else in life but despair. What a gloomy way to go. Why bother at all, one wonders. But we must recognize that if life had only despair left, then despair must be used to organize the human experience. If our assumption is correct, the alternative to despair for these men was personality disintegration. That was the only identifiable choice.

In any contest between the need to keep one's mind on a logical course and the need to worship, the motive to worship will win. I can find no other way to explain the great devotion to absurd objects, causes and movements. Witness the tremendous growth of astrology as a serious hobby of intelligent people. I believe the interest in astrology is nonsensical, at best. It makes me wonder what has happened to minds that otherwise seem capable of rational inquiry. The only explanation seems to be that man must have some system of ultimates, some object of devotion to give his life meaning and interpretation. He seems willing to worship most anything regardless of its absurdity.

The giving up of an object of worship in the face of rational insight is often most difficult. Sometimes invalid objects of worship are exposed by rational inquiry and a serious stress point in life is identified. Whole civilizations of people have been known to reject education because such a choice had to be made. Millions have lived in intellectual darkness rather than pursue inquiry which might result in the deprivation of one of life's greatest needs.

This leads us to the third premise about worship. The object of worship must be ultimately and finally valid. It must not be untrue or destructible. While even invalid objects of worship will give an organizing base to life, ultimately despair will follow if the object loses its truthfulness. Thus theology, based on sound presuppositions, is still the queen of the sciences and comparative religion is no idle parlor game.

I recently worked my way through Francis Schaeffer's book, *The God Who Is There*. The book responds to the great need to understand suppositions, logical processes and biblical evidence to establish with firmness a valid object of devotion and worship. Schaeffer clearly makes the point that when the validity question goes unsolved or unanswered, despair is the inevitable result.

Fortunately the hand of God often participates in establishing validity for Himself in the minds and hearts of people. We witnessed this fact not long ago in a tribe of jungle dwelling Indians in South America. A serious epidemic had taken several lives and left others disabled. This group of people had recently embraced Christ as Saviour but tended to revert to spiritism in the face of this disaster. Two men, at least one of whom was a professing Christian, decided to seek revenge for the illness that had gripped their tribe. To appease the spirits they thought responsible, they stalked two residents of their tribe at night and drove spears through them.

One mature Christian in the tribe apprehended one of the men and warned the assailant that God would deal seriously with him. In less than an hour the culprit was dead, having laughed derisively when warned. A somber audience of tribespeople heard the story and thanked God for protecting their new found faith, even by this drastic means.

One of the reasons for the near demise of some theological seminaries lies in their inability to clearly establish the validity of the God they worship. In one prominent seminary, it is possible to graduate with a divinity degree without ever having taken a course in biblical literature. Instead this school has devoted itself to a study of matters far less than ultimate in character. It competes with other social institutions who better relieve many of the world's social ills. Thus appearing second best as an instrument of social change and presenting an uncertain voice with regard to the validity of God, the school finds it difficult to draw men for study or to promise hope from the despair that encircles humanity. A clear and valid Saviour together with a sense of redemption ultimates in life is required if despair is not to follow.

The fourth premise is that valid worship regenerates both mind and soul. In the course of counseling and psychotherapy, I often give my clients a program of worship experience. This is not necessarily public or formal worship, but rather a personal expression. With some instruction in how to pray and how to read Scripture, I ask them to think about ideas that do not center on their illness with its accompanying drain of emotional resources.

For one seriously depressed woman I selected a series of psalms of praise that made no reference to oneself at all. I suggested that she make no mention of herself in her prayers, simply praise God, enjoy his awe and greatness and give thanks for who He is. She expressed great resistance to the idea. To enter upon such a program meant abandoning the preoccupations with self that had accompanied her spiritual exercises. She wasn't sure whether she was really ready to give up her own concerns and relate to God in this way. But she had to make her choice or realize that her therapy would become meaningless. Reluctantly, at first, but with increasing joy as she went along, she began to find her way out of her private emotional pit. Worship was regenerating her heart and mind.

I have noted that some of the most delightful people

I know are constantly in a worship frame of mind. One day I enjoyed a round of golf with a minister who was gifted in many ways: an athlete, musician and able preacher. On the first hole of our match he hit two crisp shots to the green and sank his first putt to go one under par. If you're a golfer you know what joy there is in making a birdie on the first hole! His response? He stood atop the mound that elevated the green and sang joyfully, "A Mighty Fortress Is Our God"! His immediate response even to a simple joy of life was to worship. Most people would think him silly, but I learned a lesson I never forgot. Worship removes oneself from the center of attention and replaces self with the joyful awe of God. No longer can guilt and selfishness occupy the personal stage front and center. No longer can emotional energies be sapped on miserable introspection. Worship is the mental frame of the mature person.

The fifth premise is that the only valid object of worship is the triune God, revealed in Jesus Christ. It is not my intention to present a systematic theological argument and apologetic for this statement. Rather, I want to declare with Scripture simply that in Christ all things in heaven and all things on earth will ultimately be reconciled in Him. I know of no more encompassing statement or principle that can be made. If Christ is that, then he is the worthy object of your devotion and worship. And since the statement is so final, it leaves you with a choice. The choice is to either accept it as true or as false. There is no partial acceptance or middle ground with such a statement. You must either assume truth or deny validity. It is not my statement, it is the statement of the Scriptures.

The Scriptures don't stop with this, however. They further insist that the person of Christ was *both* fully God and fully man. Who can envision or comprehend an idea like that? The processes of human mental imagery won't let it happen. So it is necessary to take a giant step of

201

faith and start believing that these statements are true. Believing means that God will then personally validate Himself for you as He did for the tribespeople spoken of earlier in this chapter. It means accepting the limits of logical thought and intellectual process. It means a willingness to begin trusting a revelation given in holy writ. When you do you will arrive at the beginning of the greatest adventure you have ever known. Worship will be the most renewing experience of your life and you'll begin a life of adventure that will take you beyond your finest expectations.